EVERYDAY KITCHEN
ESSENTIALS

by Steven Baker

TABLE OF
CONTENTS

Growing up, I always loved to help in the kitchen. I would be fascinated at the process of getting supper on the table. When I was little, I wanted to do anything and everything that I could; mixing, measuring, adding in ingredients, it didn't matter to me. I just wanted to be in the kitchen.

As I got older and was allowed to use more tools and appliances without burning down the house or killing myself, I began to experiment and cook more on my own.

Around the time I was in college and still living at my parent's house, I started watching cooking shows on TV. Up until then, the only way I learned how to cook was from watching my family cook. I was enthralled at what I saw on those shows! I learned so many things by watching the cooks, like knife skills, how to cut up a chicken, the importance of using fresh ingredients, and a plethora of other skills. Like the perfect student, I would sit there with a pen and paper and write notes on what I was learning.

After I graduated college and moved out on my own, a whole new world opened to me. I could cook what I wanted, how I wanted, and when I wanted. This is when I feel like I learned the most about cooking. Through trial and error, hits and misses, and even catching my oven on fire, I learned about cookware to make great food.

Now that I was on my own, making and spending my own money, I started to buy all kinds of

kitchen tools and gadgets I could find. I would scour the internet and cooking stores for the coolest kitchen doodads big or small. I quickly amassed a large collection of kitchenware that I ran out of room to store everything.

It was then, that I learned that while all those neat tools and appliances were fun to collect and use, I really didn't need half of them. All I needed was a handful of equipment to get any cooking job done.

As I've continued to grow and learn about cooking, I've found that there are some obvious and not-so-obvious essential kitchen equipment that I just can't live without, and that I think every kitchen should have to make life easier and home cooking more fun and enjoyable.

In this book, you'll find easy to follow recipes for each of these kitchen essentials and why they are indispensable. Some of these essentials are old-school classic tools that probably everyone has in their kitchen and some are rather new to the everyday kitchen world.

If you're just getting out on your own and starting up your first kitchen, recently gained an interest in cooking and want the right kitchen gear, or looking to update your current kitchen with some new must-haves that will make your life easier, then, let's get cooking with easy-to-follow recipes for kitchen essentials that you'll find yourself using every day.

STAND MIXER

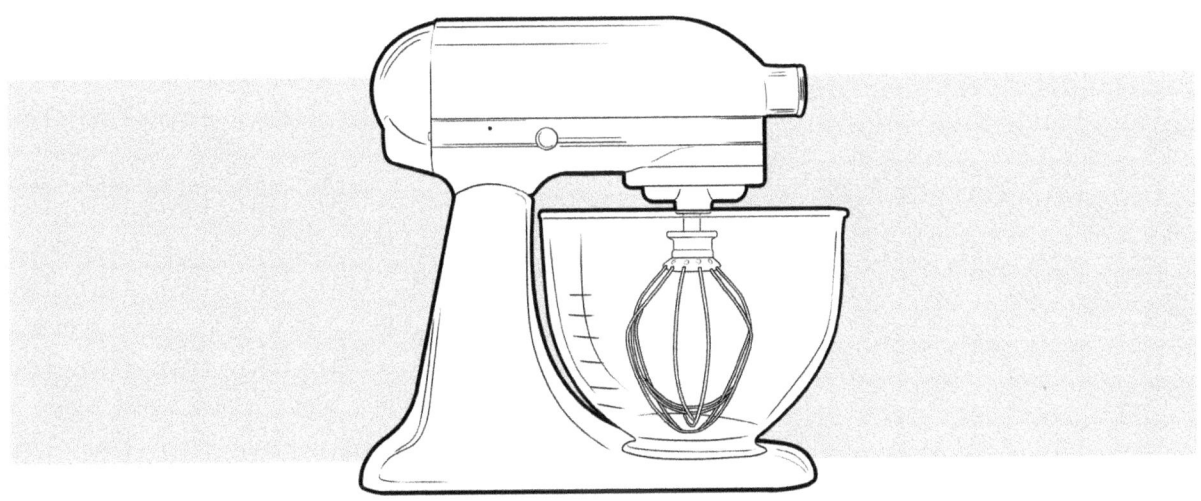

Everyone has that one household item that is near and dear to them. For me it's my stand mixer. Seriously, if mine were to stop working right now, I'd immediately get in my car and go buy a new one. That's how important this thing is to me!

What makes a stand mixer so great is the versatility. Most people think of a stand mixer as a baking tool, but you can do so much more than that. You can beat, stir, mix, mash, whip, shred, and knead hands-free with this one item. Everything from cakes, cookies, meringues for pies, pizza dough, meatloaf, cheesecake, and even bread are simplified with a stand mixer. The possibilities are endless.

You can also get a plethora of attachments such as fresh pasta roller, meat grinder, spiralizer, grain mill, slicer/shredder, and even an ice cream maker. I recommend getting a second bowl so that you can easily switch from mixing one thing and move on to the next without have to stop and wash the bowl.

There are a wide variety of brands of stand mixers out there. I use KitchenAid. A KitchenAid mixer and its attachments can get pricey, but it's completely reliable, sturdy, and durable. I've had mine for over 10 years and it's still going strong.

Like I said, stand mixers can get expensive, but I look at it as an investment. The old saying goes, "you get what you pay for", and that's definitely true with these. A good stand mixer can start out at around $300.00 and go up from there. They come in lots of different styles, sizes, and colors to fit your personal style. They look great sitting on your countertop, too. The recipes in this book are just a glimpse into what you can use a stand mixer to create. You'll also notice in different sections in this book that I use a stand mixer in other recipes...that's how much I use this thing!

CHOCOLATE CAKE WITH PEANUT BUTTER FROSTING

SERVINGS: 20-24

Who doesn't love chocolate cake? Who doesn't love peanut butter? When you put the two together, you end up with sheer heaven! The moist chocolatey cake topped with the rich, smooth peanut butter frosting is a dessert lover's dream.

INGREDIENTS

Cake:

- 2 cups all-purpose flour
- 1 teaspoon baking powder
- 1/2 teaspoon baking soda
- 1/2 teaspoon salt
- 1 tablespoon cocoa powder
- 8oz semi-sweet chocolate, roughly chopped
- 1/2 cup fresh brewed hot coffee
- 1 cup unsalted butter, room temperature
- 2 cups sugar
- 4 eggs, room temperature
- 1 teaspoon vanilla extract
- 1 cup buttermilk

Peanut Butter Frosting:

- 1 cup unsalted butter, room temperature
- 1 cup smooth peanut butter
- 1 teaspoon vanilla extract
- 1/2 teaspoon salt
- 3 cups confectioners' sugar
- 1/4 cup heavy cream

DIRECTIONS

- Preheat the oven to 350 degrees. Grease 3 9" cake pans and line with parchment paper.
- Sift together the flour, baking powder, baking soda, salt, and cocoa powder into a large bowl and set aside.
- In a small bowl, whisk together the chocolate and hot coffee until the chocolate is smooth. Set aside.
- In the bowl of a stand mixer fitted with the paddle attachment, beat the butter and sugar together until creamy, about 4 minutes. Scrape the sides of the bowl as needed. With the mixer on low, add the eggs one at a time until well incorporated. Mix in the vanilla extract and chocolate-coffee mixture. Slowly add the flour mixture and buttermilk a little at a time starting and ending with the flour mixture until well incorporated.
- Divide the batter between the cake pans and smooth out the tops with the back of a spoon. Bake for 30-35 minutes until a toothpick comes out clean. Remove the pans from the oven and let cool for 15 minutes, then turn the cake layers onto a wire rack to cool completely.
- For the frosting, beat the butter and peanut butter in the bowl of a stand mixer fitted with the paddle attachment until smooth, about 3 minutes. Mix in the vanilla extract and salt until combined. Add in the confectioners' sugar a little at a time until incorporated. Beat in the heavy cream until smooth. Apply the frosting to the cooled cake.

FUNFETTI CAKE

SERVINGS: 20-24

This colorful, homemade birthday cake is perfect for any party...kid or adult!

INGREDIENTS

Cake:

- 3 cups cake flour
- 1 tablespoon baking powder
- 1 teaspoon baking soda
- 1/2 teaspoon salt
- 4 eggs, separated, room temperature
- 1-1/2 cups sugar, divided
- 1 cup unsalted butter, room temperature
- 1 tablespoon vanilla extract
- 1-1/2 cups buttermilk
- 1/2 cup rainbow sprinkles

Frosting:

- 1-1/4 cups unsalted butter, room temperature
- 5 cups confectioners' sugar
- 2 teaspoons vanilla extract
- 1/4 cup heavy cream
- 1/2 cup rainbow sprinkles

DIRECTIONS

- Preheat the oven to 350 degrees. Grease (3) 9" cake pans and line with parchment paper.

- Sift together the flour, baking powder, baking soda, and salt into a large bowl and set aside.

- In the bowl of a stand mixer fitted with the whisk attachment, beat the egg whites and 1/4 cup sugar until soft peaks form, about 3 minutes. Scrape the egg whites into a separate bowl and set aside.

- In the bowl of a stand mixer fitted with the paddle attachment, beat the butter and 1-1/4 cup sugar together until creamy, about 4 minutes. Scrape the sides of the bowl as needed. With the mixer on low, add the egg yolks one at a time until well incorporated. Mix in the vanilla extract. Slowly add in the flour mixture and buttermilk a little at a time starting and ending with the flour mixture until well incorporated. Gently, fold in egg whites and rainbow sprinkles until combined.

- Divide the batter between the cake pans and smooth out the tops with the back of a spoon. Bake for 30-35 minutes until a toothpick comes out clean. Remove the pans from the oven and let cool for 15 minutes, then transfer cake layers to a wire rack to cool completely.

- For the frosting, in the stand mixer fitted with the paddle attachment, beat the butter until smooth, about 3 minutes. With the mixer on low, add the confectioners' sugar a little at a time until incorporated. Beat in the vanilla extract and heavy cream until smooth. Fold in the rainbow sprinkles. Apply the frosting to the cooled cake.

PIG-PICKIN' CAKE

SERVINGS: 20-24

You'll find this summertime favorite dessert at any BBQ or potluck you go to in the South. This fluffy and fruity cake uses simple ingredients and is a snap to make.

INGREDIENTS

Cake:

- 3 cups cake flour
- 1 tablespoon baking powder
- 1 teaspoon salt
- 12 tablespoons unsalted butter, room temperature
- 1-1/2 cups sugar
- 3 egg yolks, room temperature
- 1 teaspoon vanilla extract
- zest of 2 oranges
- 1/2 cup orange juice, freshly squeezed
- 1 cup whole milk

Icing:

- 2 cups heavy cream
- 1 teaspoon vanilla extract
- 1 cup confectioners' sugar
- 1 8oz can crushed pineapple with juice

DIRECTIONS

- Pre-heat the oven to 350 degrees. Grease 3 9-inch cake pans and line the bottoms with parchment paper.

- Sift together the flour, baking powder, and salt into a medium-sized bowl and set aside.

- In the bowl of a stand mixer fitted with the paddle attachment, beat the butter and sugar until creamed, about 5 minutes. Add each egg yolk one at a time until incorporated. Add in the vanilla extract, orange zest, and orange juice until well mixed. Slowly add in the flour mixture and milk a little at a time starting and ending with the flour mixture.

- Evenly pour the batter into the cake pans and smooth out the tops. Bake for 20-25 minutes until a toothpick comes out clean. Remove the cake pans from the oven and let cool for 15 minutes, then turn out on a wire rack to cool completely.

- For the icing, beat the heavy cream in the stand mixer fitted with the whisk attachment until the cream begins to thicken. Mix in the vanilla extract and confectioners' sugar until stiff peaks form, then fold in the crushed pineapple. Apply the icing to the cake. Serve immediately or store in the refrigerator.

CARAMEL CAKE

SERVINGS: 20-24

A Southern classic! The rich caramel icing is the perfect complement to the moist buttery cake.

TOOLS OF THE TRADE

Rubber Spatulas: There never seems to be enough of these. Scrape, stir, fold, mix...I can never have enough of these babies!

INGREDIENTS

Cake:

- 2-1/2 cups cake flour
- 1 tablespoon baking powder
- 1 teaspoon baking soda
- 1 teaspoon salt
- 3 eggs, separated, room temperature
- 1/4 teaspoon cream of tartar
- 12 tablespoons unsalted butter, room temperature
- 1-1/2 cups sugar
- 3 egg yolks, room temperature
- 1/2 cup sour cream
- 2 teaspoons vanilla extract
- 2 tablespoons vegetable oil
- 1 cup buttermilk

Frosting:

- 12 tablespoons unsalted butter
- 1-1/2 cups brown sugar
- 1/2 cup whole milk
- 1-1/2 teaspoons vanilla extract
- 2 cups confectioners' sugar, sifted

DIRECTIONS

- Preheat the oven to 350 degrees. Grease (2) 9in cake pans and line with parchment paper.

- Sift together the cake flour, baking powder, baking soda, and salt into a large bowl and set aside.

- In the bowl of a stand mixer fitted with the whisk attachment, beat the egg whites and cream of tartar on high until soft peaks form. Transfer beaten egg whites to a separate bowl and set aside.

- In the bowl of a stand mixer fitted with the paddle attachment, beat the butter and sugar until creamed, stopping every so often to scrape down the sides of the bowl, about 5 minutes. Beat in the 6 egg yolks one at a time until well combined. Add the sour cream, vanilla extract, and vegetable oil and beat until combined. On low speed, slowly add in the flour mixture and buttermilk a little at a time, starting and ending with the flour mixture. Using a rubber spatula, fold in the egg whites into the batter.

- Evenly distribute the batter into the cake pans. Bake for 25-30 minutes until a toothpick comes out clean. Remove the pans from the oven and cool for 10 minutes, then turn the cakes over onto a wire rack to cool completely.

- For the frosting, add butter and brown sugar to a medium sauce pan over medium heat. Stir constantly until the butter is melted and the mixture begins to boil. Stir in the milk and bring back to a vigorous boil, then remove from heat. Stir in the vanilla extract. Whisk in the confectioners' sugar 1/2 cup at a time. Set the frosting aside to cool until spreadable, about 1 hour. Apply frosting to the cake layers and set the cake aside for the frosting to set completely.

ICEBOX CINNAMON SWIRL COOKIES

SERVINGS: 18-20

These slice and bake cookies are crisp on the outside and soft and chewy on the inside. Perfect to make ahead and store in the freezer to bake whenever you want.

INGREDIENTS

- 3 cups all-purpose flour
- 1 teaspoon baking powder
- 1/2 teaspoon baking soda
- 1/4 teaspoon salt
- 1 cup unsalted butter, room temperature
- 3/4 cup plus 1/2 tablespoon white sugar, divided
- 1/4 cup brown sugar
- 2 eggs
- 2 teaspoons vanilla extract
- 1 tablespoon ground cinnamon

DIRECTIONS

- Over a medium bowl, sift together the flour, baking powder, baking soda, and salt and set aside.

- In the bowl of a stand mixer fitted with the paddle attachment, beat the butter, 3/4 cup white sugar, and brown sugar until creamy, about 5 minutes. Mix in the eggs and vanilla extract. With the mixer on low, slowly mix in the flour mixture until the dough comes together.

- Dump the dough in the center of a piece of plastic wrap and wrap the dough to form a disc. Chill in the refrigerator for 30 minutes to allow the dough to firm up.

- Mix the cinnamon and 1/2 tablespoon of sugar together in a small bowl. Roll out the dough between 2 sheets of parchment paper to approximately 1/4-inch in thickness. Sprinkle the cinnamon-sugar mixture all over the top of the chilled dough.

- Roll the dough into a tight log and then smear the end seam with a small amount of water to seal. Tightly roll the log in plastic wrap and refrigerate for 4 hours. Keep in the refrigerator for up to one week or in the freezer for 3 months (place in refrigerator overnight to thaw if using from freezer).

- To bake the cookies: preheat the oven to 375 degrees and line a baking sheet with parchment paper. Cut the cookies into 1/2-inch slices and bake for 12-15 minutes until the cookies are golden brown around the edges.

CHOCOLATE CHIP COOKIES

SERVINGS: 18-20

Chocolate chip cookies are my all-time favorite dessert. The slightly crispy outside with the gooey center makes my mouth water! These were one of the first things that I made for my husband and to this day, he always asks me to make "those cookies like you made when we first met."

INGREDIENTS

- 2-3/4 cups all-purpose flour
- 1 teaspoon baking soda
- 1 teaspoon salt
- 1 cup unsalted butter, room temperature
- 1 cup brown sugar
- 1/2 cup white sugar
- 2 eggs
- 1-1/2 teaspoons vanilla extract
- 1-1/2 cups chocolate chips

DIRECTIONS

- Preheat the oven to 350 degrees and line a baking sheet with parchment paper.
- Over a medium bowl, sift together the flour, baking soda, and salt and set aside.
- In the bowl of a stand mixer fitted with the paddle attachment, beat the butter, brown sugar, and white sugar until smooth. Mix in the eggs and vanilla extract until combined. With the mixer on low, slowly add in the flour mixture until the dough comes together, then fold in the chocolate chips.
- Drop the dough onto the baking sheet with a small ice cream scoop, about 2 tablespoons of dough per cookie. Bake for 9-11 minutes until the cookies are golden brown around the edges.

CORN MUFFINS

SERVINGS: 12

These tender and sweet muffins go perfectly with chili, ribs, or even served as a dessert.

INGREDIENTS

- 1 cup all-purpose flour
- 1 cup yellow cornmeal
- 1/2 cup sugar
- 1 tablespoon baking powder
- 1 teaspoon salt
- 2 eggs, beaten
- 1 cup whole milk
- 4 tablespoons unsalted butter, melted
- 1/4 cup honey
- 2 tablespoons vegetable oil

DIRECTIONS

- Preheat the oven to 400 degrees. Line a muffin pan with paper liners.

- Add the flour, cornmeal, sugar, baking powder, and salt to the bowl of a stand mixer fitted with the paddle attachment. Mix on low until well combined.

- In a separate medium-sized bowl, whisk together the eggs, milk, melted butter, honey, and vegetable oil. Add to the dry mixture and mix on low until just combined. Don't over mix or the muffins with be tough.

- Evenly divide the batter into the muffin pan. Bake for 15 minutes until the corn muffins are golden brown. Top with melted butter or honey.

LEMON MERINGUE PIE

SERVINGS: 10-12

This sweet and tangy pie is topped with a fluffy meringue that has just a hint of lemon.
With the help of a stand mixer, you'll have a stunning meringue in minutes.

INGREDIENTS

Pie

- 1 unbaked pie crust (pg 36)
- 1-1/4 cups sugar
- 1/3 cup corn starch
- 1/4 teaspoon salt
- 1-1/4 cups water
- 5 egg yolks, beaten (save whites for meringue)
- 1 tablespoon lemon zest
- 1/2 cup lemon juice (about 3 lemons)
- 2 tablespoons unsalted butter

Meringue:

- 5 egg whites
- 1/4 cup sugar
- 1/2 teaspoon salt
- 1/4 teaspoon lemon extract
- 1/4 teaspoon cream of tartar

DIRECTIONS

- Preheat the oven to 350 degrees.

- For the pie crust: Roll out the pie dough on a floured board into a thin circle that's 1-inch larger than the pie dish. Transfer the dough to the pie dish and cut off any excess dough on the edge. Crimp the edge with your fingers or a fork. Line the pie crust with buttered aluminum foil with the buttered side down. Fill the pie shell with pie weights or dried beans and bake for 15 minutes. When done, remove from oven, discard aluminum foil and pie weights. Set aside.

- For the filling: add the sugar, corn starch, salt, and water to a medium-sized pan over medium heat. Cook for 5-6 minutes until the mixture thickens. Remove from heat and slowly whisk in the beaten egg yolks. Place the pan back on the heat and cook until bubbly, about 1 minute, then remove from heat. Stir in the lemon zest, lemon juice, and butter until combined. Pour the filling into the pie shell.

- For the meringue: add the egg whites, sugar, salt, lemon extract, and cream of tartar to the bowl of a stand mixer fitted with the whisk attachment. Beat on high speed until stiff peaks form, about 3-4 minutes.

- Turn the oven temperature down to 325. Spread the meringue over the pie, then bake for 20-25 minutes until the meringue turns golden brown. Let cool before slicing.

CHEESECAKE BROWNIES

SERVINGS: 12

A layer of cheesecake. A layer of brownie. Is there anything better?

INGREDIENTS

Brownie Batter:

- 1 cup all-purpose flour
- 1/4 cup cocoa powder
- 1 tablespoon baking powder
- 1/4 teaspoon salt
- 1/2 cup unsalted butter
- 12oz semi-sweet chocolate, roughly chopped
- 1 cup sugar
- 2 tablespoons brewed coffee
- 1 teaspoon vanilla extract
- 3 eggs

Cheesecake Batter:

- 2 eggs
- 1 tablespoon lemon juice
- 1 teaspoon vanilla extract
- 1 tablespoon sour cream
- 1 tablespoon all-purpose flour
- 1/2 cup sugar
- Pinch of salt
- 16oz cream cheese, room temperature

DIRECTIONS

- Preheat the oven to 350 degrees and grease a 9x9in baking pan lined with parchment paper.

- For the brownie batter, sift together the flour, cocoa powder, baking powder, and salt over a medium-sized bowl and set aside.

- Add the butter and chocolate to a double boiler and heat until melted and smooth.

- In a large bowl, stir together the melted chocolate with the sugar until combined. Stir in the coffee and vanilla extract. Once the mixture is slightly cooled, stir in the eggs until incorporated. Stir in the flour mixture until well combined, then pour batter into the pan, reserving 1/2 cup.

- For the cheesecake batter, add the eggs to the bowl of a stand mixer fitted with the paddle attachment and beat for 1 minute. Add in the lemon juice, vanilla extract, and sour cream and mix until incorporated. Mix in the flour, sugar, and salt until combined. Add the cream cheese and beat until just combined. Pour the cheesecake batter into the pan over top of the brownie batter.

- Add 1 tablespoon of hot water to the reserved brownie batter to thin the batter out. Place the brownie batter in dots over top of the cheesecake batter. With a skewer, swirl the brownie batter to mix with the cheesecake batter to create a marble look.

- Bake at 350 for 10 minutes, then reduce the heat to 325 and bake for 30-35 minutes until a toothpick inserted into the center comes out clean. The center will be slightly jiggly. Set at room temperature until cooled completely, then slice. Store in airtight container in the refrigerator for up to 4 days.

TIRAMISU CHEESECAKE

TOOLS OF THE TRADE

Multiple Measuring Cups/Spoons: measure dry and wet ingredients.

SERVINGS: 10-12

I used to think you couldn't get any better than just plain ole' cheesecake. Boy was I wrong! The coffee-soaked ladyfingers that sit smack dab in the center of this delectable cheesecake, topped with a rich mascarpone cream topping is to die for!

INGREDIENTS

Crust:
- 25 chocolate sandwich cookies, ground into crumbs
- 2 teaspoons espresso powder
- 6 tablespoons unsalted butter, melted

Filling:
- 4 eggs, separated
- 1-1/2 cups sugar, divided
- 2 teaspoons vanilla extract
- 1-1/4 cups brewed strong coffee, cooled
- 1/3 cup mascarpone cheese
- 2 tablespoons all-purpose flour, sifted
- 1/2 teaspoon salt
- 24oz cream cheese, room temperature
- 10-12 ladyfinger cookies

Topping:
- 1 cup heavy cream
- 2 teaspoons vanilla extract
- 1/3 cup mascarpone cheese
- 1/2 tablespoon cocoa powder

DIRECTIONS

- Preheat the oven to 350 degrees. Line the sides of a 9-inch springform pan with parchment paper and grease bottom.

- For the crust, add the cookie crumbs, espresso powder, and melted butter to the springform pan and stir to combine. Press the mixture evenly on the bottom and up the sides of the pan. Place in the refrigerator to chill.

- In the bowl of a stand mixer fitted with the whisk attachment, beat the egg whites and 1/4 cup sugar until soft peaks form. Transfer the egg whites to another bowl and set aside.

- Add the egg yolks to the mixer bowl and beat for 1 minute. Mix in the vanilla extract, 1/4 cup coffee, and mascarpone cheese until well incorporated. Beat in the remaining 1-1/4 cup sugar, flour, and salt until combined. Add the cream cheese and mix until smooth. With a rubber spatula, gently fold in the egg whites until well mixed.

- Pour half of the batter into the springform pan. Dip the lady fingers into the remaining coffee, then place on top of the batter in the pan. Pour the rest of the batter into the pan and smooth out the top with the back of a spoon. Lightly bang the pan on the counter to remove any air bubbles.

- Bake for 15 minutes, reduce heat to 200 degrees, then bake for 2 hours until the center is firm. Turn the oven off and let the cheesecake sit for 3 hours. Remove from the oven and let sit at room temperature for 1 hour. Refrigerate overnight before removing the cheesecake from the pan and slicing.

- Topping: in the bowl of a stand mixer fitted with the whisk attachment, beat heavy cream and vanilla extract until stiff peaks form. Fold in mascarpone cheese. Spread over the top of the cheesecake and dust with the cocoa powder.

FRIED CHEESE RAVIOLI

MAKES: About 30

These crispy, cheesy ravioli will quickly become a family favorite.
Perfect to make ahead and store in the freezer.

INGREDIENTS

- 1 cup ricotta cheese
- 1 cup mozzarella cheese
- 1/2 cup Parmesan cheese
- 1/2 teaspoon salt
- 1/4 teaspoon black pepper
- 1 teaspoon fresh basil, chopped
- 1/8 teaspoon nutmeg
- Zest of 1 lemon
- 1lb pasta dough (pg 27)
- 4 cups vegetable oil
- 2 eggs, whisked
- 1 cup Italian bread crumbs
- Marinara sauce for dipping

DIRECTIONS

- In a large bowl, mix together the ricotta cheese, mozzarella cheese, Parmesan cheese, salt, pepper, basil, nutmeg, and lemon zest until combined. Set aside.

- Using the pasta roller attachment for a stand mixer, roll out the pasta dough for ravioli into flat sheets. Place the sheets of pasta on a flat surface dusted with flour. Using a ravioli cutter, lightly make indentions on the pasta. Add a small spoonful of filling to the center of the indention. Dip your finger in water and then run your finger around the edge of each indention. Place the next sheet of pasta over the first sheet and lightly press around the filling to seal the pasta and remove any air. Take the ravioli cutter and firmly press around the filling to cut out each ravioli. Place the ravioli on a baking sheet lined with parchment paper. Repeat for the rest of the pasta sheets.

- Add the vegetable oil to a large pot over medium-high heat.

- Add the eggs and 1 tablespoon water to a shallow bowl. Add the bread crumbs to another shallow bowl. Dredge the ravioli in the egg mixture, then the bread crumbs.

- Once the oil is hot (about 325 degrees) add the ravioli and cook in batches 1 minute each side. Serve hot with marinara sauce.

FRESH PASTA DOUGH

MAKES: 1lb of Pasta

Pasta made from scratch sounds daunting, but it's actually very easy and fun to make, plus you probably already have all the ingredients that you need. Probably the hardest part of making fresh pasta is rolling the dough out to the desired thinness, but that is made so much easier with the pasta attachment for a stand mixer. Whether you're making lasagna noodles, ravioli, or spaghetti, you'll be amazed at the difference fresh pasta makes. It's important to weigh the ingredients so that your dough will be the proper texture.

INGREDIENTS

- 300 grams all-purpose or 00 flour (approx. 2-1/2 cups)
- 185 grams extra large eggs (approx. 2 eggs + 1 yolk)
- 1 teaspoon salt

DIRECTIONS

- Weigh out 300 grams of flour and 185 grams eggs. If needed, add water to the eggs to equal 185 grams.

- Add the eggs, flour, and salt to the bowl of a stand mixer fitted with the dough hook attachment. Mix on medium-low speed until the dough comes together, about 2 minutes. Dump dough onto a smooth surface and hand-knead for 8-10 minutes until the dough is smooth. Form the dough into a ball, sprinkle with flour, and wrap in plastic wrap. Refrigerate for 30 minutes.

- To roll out the pasta, fit the stand mixer with the pasta attachment and flour the pasta roller to prevent the dough from sticking. Divide the dough into quarters. Working with a quarter of the dough at a time, flatten the dough with your hand and run through the roller on low speed on the first setting. Fold the dough onto its self to form a square, then run through the roller again. Repeat 3 more times.

- Next, increase the setting and run the dough through the roller twice with each setting. Repeat, increasing the setting until you reach the desired thickness. Cut dough in half once it begins to get too long to handle. Repeat for each quarter of dough.

- Stop at level 5 for ribbon pasta such as spaghetti or linguine and stop at level 6 for flat pasta such as ravioli.

- To cook the pasta, bring a large pot of salted water to a boil. Add the pasta and cook for 1 minute.

PIZZA DOUGH

MAKES: 2 Pizzas

Easy no-fuss pizza dough...what could be better?

INGREDIENTS

- 2-1/4 teaspoons (1 package) active dry yeast
- 1-1/2 teaspoons sugar
- 2 tablespoons olive oil
- 1-1/2 cups warm water (105-115 degrees)
- 1 teaspoon salt
- 3-1/4 cup all-purpose flour

DIRECTIONS

- Add the yeast, sugar, olive oil, and warm water to the bowl of a stand mixer and let sit for 5 minutes.

- Add the salt and flour to the bowl and then knead with the dough hook attachment for 8 minutes on medium-high until the dough is smooth and elastic.

- Transfer the dough to a large bowl brushed with olive oil (the dough will be very sticky). Turn the dough over in the bowl to cover with olive oil. Cover the bowl with a kitchen towel and set in a warm place for 45 minutes to 1 hour until the dough doubles in size. Dump the dough out onto a floured surface and cut into 2 equal halves.

- Lightly dust the dough and your hands with flour. Press the dough out to form a small disc then stretch the dough out to the shape of the pan you are using.

- Freeze the dough for up to one month. Make sure the dough is at room temperature before using.

FOOD PROCESSOR

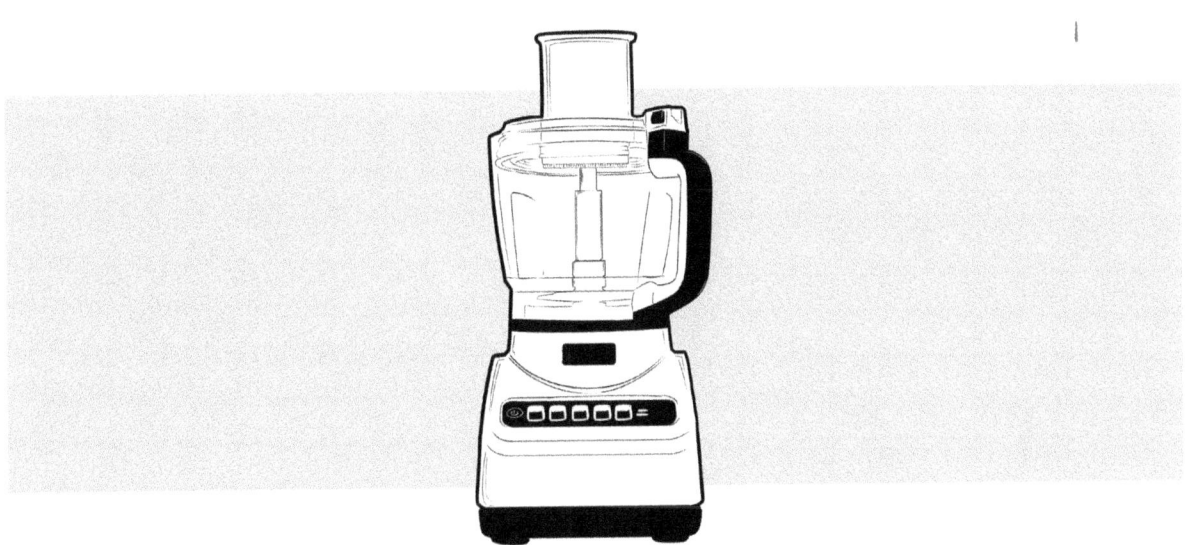

In today's fast-paced world, most people don't have the time or energy for preparing meals. Everything is done to make cooking easier and faster in today's kitchen and a food processor is one of the main tools to help accomplish this. They are about as multi-functional as it gets.

Food processors are small, powerful, and easy-to-clean appliances that help with everyday cooking by cutting back on the use of utensils.

A food processor can cut a lot of time in prepping food. You can chop, grind, puree, and mince ingredients in no time. You can also use it to shred blocks of cheese in seconds; no more grating cheese by hand!

They can do a lot more than process food. You can make sauces, batters, and doughs in a matter of minutes. They will expand your cooking to whole new horizons.

My favorite thing to make in the food processor is dough for pies. Sure, it's easy to just buy a frozen pie crust, but there's just something about a made-from-scratch pie crust that makes pies taste so much better. With the help of the food processor, you can have a buttery flakey pie crust made in no time.

My absolute least favorite thing about cooking is have to clean up afterwards. Sometimes I will not cook and get take-out just so I won't have to clean up the mess. That's my most favorite thing about my food processor, how easy it is to clean! After I'm done using it, I simply throw it in the dishwasher and keep on going.

With a food processor, you can make dishes from sweet to savory and everything in between. You'll find It will quickly become your best friend in the kitchen!

BRAD'S KENTUCKY CHOCOLATE PIE

SERVINGS: 10-12

My husband Brad has cooked me two things since we met: chicken casserole and his version of a Derby Pie. His family is from the great state of Kentucky and this dessert is always a family favorite.

INGREDIENTS

- 1 unbaked pie crust (pg 36)
- 1/2 cup all-purpose flour
- 1 tablespoon cocoa powder
- 1 cup sugar
- pinch of salt
- 1 cup chocolate chips
- 1 cup pecans, roughly chopped
- 2 eggs, lightly beaten
- 1 teaspoon vanilla extract
- 2 tablespoons bourbon
- 1/2 cup unsalted butter, melted

DIRECTIONS

- Preheat the oven to 350 degrees.
- Roll out the pie dough on a floured board into a thin circle that's 1-inch larger than the pie dish. Transfer the dough to the pie dish and cut off any excess dough on the edge. Crimp the edge with your fingers or a fork.
- Sift together the flour and cocoa powder into a medium-sized bowl. Add the sugar, salt, chocolate chips, pecans, eggs, vanilla extract, bourbon, and butter and stir together until combined.
- Pour the batter into the pie plate and bake for 40 minutes until the pie is set. Allow to cool slightly before cutting.

TOOLS OF THE TRADE

Pie Shield: prevent the edges of the crust from browning faster that the rest of the crust. Perfectly baked pie every time!

ROASTED LEG OF LAMB

SERVINGS: 8-10

With the help of a food processor, you can have this savory rub ready in minutes for this no-stress, succulent meal.

INGREDIENTS

- Cloves from 1 whole head of garlic
- 2 tablespoons fresh rosemary, chopped
- 1 tablespoon fresh thyme, chopped
- 1 tablespoon salt
- 1/2 tablespoon black pepper
- 1/2 tablespoon paprika
- 1 teaspoon dried oregano
- Zest and juice from 1 lemon
- 1/4 cup olive oil
- 4-5lb leg of lamb

DIRECTIONS

- Preheat the oven to 350 degrees. Place the rack in the lower 1/3 of the oven.
- Add the garlic, rosemary, thyme, salt, pepper, paprika, oregano, lemon zest, and juice to the bowl of a food processor. With the processor on high, pour the olive oil down the feed tube and process until the mixture is pureed.
- Spread the rub all over the lamb and place on a rack in a roasting pan. Roast in the oven for 1-1/2 - 2 hours until the internal temperature reads 135 degrees. Remove from the oven and wrap the lamb in aluminum foil and let sit for 15-20 minutes. Slice and serve warm.

SUGAR COOKIES

MAKES: Approximately 30 Cookies

Sugar cookies that are a snap to make...perfect for Christmas cookies!

INGREDIENTS

- 2-1/4 cups all-purpose flour
- 1 teaspoon baking powder
- 1/2 teaspoon baking soda
- 1/2 teaspoon salt
- 1 cup cold unsalted butter, diced
- 1-1/4 cup sugar, divided
- 1 egg
- 2 teaspoons vanilla extract

DIRECTIONS

- Preheat the oven to 350 degrees. Line 2 baking sheets with parchment paper.

- Sift together flour, baking powder, baking soda, and salt into a medium-sized bowl and set aside.

- In the bowl of a food processor, add butter and 1 cup sugar and pulse several times until the butter is the size of peas. Add the egg and vanilla extract and process until combined. Add the flour mixture and process until the dough comes together.

- Add 1/4 cup sugar to a small bowl. Take about 1-1/2 tablespoons of the dough and roll into a ball, then toss the ball in the bowl of sugar to cover the ball of dough completely. Place the dough on the baking sheet. Repeat for the rest of the dough placing the dough balls about 2 inches apart from each other on the baking sheet, as the dough will flatten and spread as the cookies bake.

- Bake for 18-20 minutes until the edges set. Let the cookies cool for 5 minutes on the baking sheet.

PIE CRUST DOUGH

MAKES: 1 Pie Crust

Pie crust dough is surprisingly easy to make and is made even more simple with a food processor. In no time, you'll have a flakey, made-from-scratch pie crust to elevate any dessert.

INGREDIENTS

- 1-1/2 cups all-purpose flour
- 1 tablespoon sugar
- 1/4 teaspoon salt
- 2 tablespoons cold vegetable shortening
- 1/2 cup cold unsalted butter, diced into small cubes
- 1/4 cup ice water

DIRECTIONS

- In the bowl of a food processor, add the flour, sugar, and salt and pulse to mix. Next, add the vegetable shortening and butter and pulse several times until the butter is the size of peas. With the processor on high, pour the iced water down the feed tube and process until the ball of dough forms.

- Dump the dough out onto a floured board and form into a disc. Wrap the dough in plastic wrap and chill in the refrigerator for at least 30 minutes before rolling out.

CAULIFLOWER PIZZA CRUST

MAKES: (1) 9-10" Pizza Crust

A crispy, healthy, low-carb alternative to regular pizza crust

INGREDIENTS

- 1 head cauliflower, cut into florets
- 2/3 cup Parmesan cheese
- 1 teaspoon fresh thyme, chopped
- 1 teaspoon garlic powder
- 1/2 teaspoon dried oregano
- 1/2 teaspoon salt
- 2 eggs
- 1/2 cup pizza sauce
- 1 cup mozzarella cheese

DIRECTIONS

- Working in batches, add the cauliflower florets to the bowl of a food processor and process until the cauliflower is the consistency of rice.

- Steam the cauliflower for 5 minutes, then allow to cool to room temperature. Next, place the cauliflower in a cheesecloth and squeeze until all of the liquid is drained off.

- Pre-heat the oven to 425 degrees. Line a pizza pan with parchment paper.

- Add the cauliflower, Parmesan cheese, thyme, garlic powder, oregano, salt, and eggs to a large bowl and stir to combine. Form into a ball and transfer to the pizza pan. Press and spread the mixture to form the crust 9 to 10 inches in diameter. Place in the oven and cook for 20 minutes.

- Remove the pan from the oven and spread the pizza sauce and mozzarella cheese over the crust, then add any toppings to the pizza that you'd like. Place the pan back in the oven for 10 minutes. Turn the oven to broil for 1-2 minutes until the cheese is slightly browned and bubbly.

GLAZED HAM

SERVINGS: 12-14

Luscious sticky glaze slathered all over a juicy tender ham is perfect for any holiday meal.

INGREDIENTS

- 1 (8-10lb) fully-cooked, bone-in spiral-cut ham
- 1 cup dark brown sugar
- 4 garlic cloves
- 1/4 cup honey
- 1/4 cup apple cider vinegar
- 2 tablespoons Dijon mustard
- 1/2 teaspoon cloves
- 1/4 teaspoon ground cinnamon
- Zest from 1 orange

DIRECTIONS

- Preheat the oven to 325 degrees. Place the ham on a rack in a large roasting pan. Cover the ham with aluminum foil and add 1 cup of water to the pan. Bake for 2 hours.

- For the glaze, add brown sugar, garlic cloves, honey, apple cider vinegar, Dijon mustard, cloves, cinnamon, and orange zest to the bowl of a food processor. Pulse several times until processed. Pour the glaze into a medium sauce pan and simmer over low heat for 15 minutes.

- Remove the ham from the oven and discard the aluminum foil. Pour the glaze over the ham and return the pan to the oven. Cook for 45 minutes uncovered, basting every 10 minutes with pan drippings.

- Remove the ham from the oven and let cool for 10-15 minutes. Serve hot or at room temperature.

COLESLAW

SERVINGS: 10-12

This classic Southern side dish goes perfectly with any meal. Shred or chop the cabbage in no time with the food processor…no more shredding by hand!

INGREDIENTS

- 1 head cabbage, quartered
- 1 cup mayonnaise
- 3 tablespoons yellow mustard
- Juice from 1 lemon
- 1 tablespoon white wine vinegar
- 2 tablespoons sugar
- 1-1/2 teaspoons black pepper

DIRECTIONS

Working in batches, chop or shred the cabbage in the food processor, then transfer to a large bowl. Add in the mayonnaise, mustard, lemon juice, white wine vinegar, sugar, and pepper and stir until combined. Serve cold or at room temperature.

HUMMUS

MAKES: 2 Cups

This Middle Eastern dip is smooth, savory, and so easy to make.

INGREDIENTS

- (2) 15.5oz cans chickpeas
- Juice from 2 lemons
- 2 garlic cloves
- 1/3 cup tahini
- 1/2 teaspoon cumin
- 1/2 teaspoon salt
- 1/4 cup olive oil
- Paprika
- Fresh parsley, roughly chopped

DIRECTIONS

Drain the chickpeas, reserving 2 tablespoons of the liquid. In the bowl of a food processor, add the chickpeas, reserved chickpea liquid, lemon juice, garlic cloves, tahini, cumin, salt, and olive oil. Process until it forms a paste, scraping down the sides as needed. Sprinkle with paprika and parsley.

PESTO

MAKES: 1 Cup

Homemade pesto is the perfect complement to pasta, bread, pizza, and pretty much anything else you can think of. Made from fresh, summertime ingredients, this will make an instant and tasty meal.

INGREDIENTS

- 2 cups fresh basil
- 1/2 cup fresh cilantro (optional)
- 1/3 cup pine nuts or walnuts
- 1/2 cup Parmesan cheese, shredded
- 3 garlic cloves
- 2 tablespoons lemon juice
- 1/4 teaspoon salt
- 1/4 teaspoon black pepper
- 1/2 cup olive oil

DIRECTIONS

Add the basil, cilantro (if using), and nuts to the bowl of a food processor and pulse several times. Add the Parmesan cheese, garlic, lemon juice, salt, and pepper. With the processor on high, pour the olive oil down the feed tube and process for about 2-3 minutes until desired consistency, stopping to scrape down the sides of the bowl ever so often. Serve immediately or store in an airtight container in the refrigerator for 4-5 days.

Photo shown is of the Restaurant-Style Salsa

RESTAURANT-STYLE SALSA

MAKES: 4-1/2 cups

If dog is man's best friend and diamonds are a girl's best friend, then chips and salsa are everyone's best friend! Fresh restaurant-style salsa is made super easy with a food processor.

INGREDIENTS

- 28oz can whole tomatoes
- 2 Roma tomatoes, roughly diced
- 1/2 cup red onion, roughly diced
- 1 jalapeño pepper, roughly diced (remove seeds for less heat)
- 2 garlic cloves
- 1/3 cup fresh cilantro
- 2 tablespoons lime juice
- 4.5oz can green chiles
- 1/4 teaspoon salt
- 1/4 teaspoon black pepper
- 1/4 teaspoon cumin
- 1/4 teaspoon sugar

DIRECTIONS

Place all ingredients in a food processor and process until desired consistency.

ROASTED TOMATILLO SALSA

MAKES: 2 cups

Fresh salsa with the volume turned way up! The flavor really comes alive in this classic Mexican dish with the roasted tomatillos.

INGREDIENTS

- 1lb fresh tomatillos, husks and stems removed
- 1 poblano pepper
- 1 jalapeño pepper
- 2 tablespoons olive oil
- 1/2 cup onion, chopped
- 1 garlic clove
- 1 teaspoon salt
- 2 tablespoons fresh lime juice
- 1/2 cup fresh cilantro, roughly chopped

DIRECTIONS

- Place the tomatillos, poblano pepper, and jalapeño pepper on a baking sheet and toss together with the olive oil. Broil in the oven for 8-10 minutes until the tomatillos and peppers begin to char. Remove from the oven and set aside to cool. Remove the skins from the tomatillos and peppers.

- Add the tomatillos, poblano pepper, jalapeño pepper, onion, garlic, salt, lime juice, and cilantro to the bowl of a food processor and process until desired consistency.

TOMATO BISQUE

MAKES: Approximately 2 quarts

This creamy, hearty take on classic tomato soup is smooth and delicious. Perfect on a cold day paired with grilled cheese sandwiches!

INGREDIENTS

- 4 tablespoons unsalted butter
- 1 medium onion, diced
- 2 celery stalks, diced
- 4 garlic cloves, minced
- 3 tablespoons all-purpose flour
- 3 cups chicken stock
- 1 cup tomato juice

- 28oz can crushed tomatoes
- 1 teaspoon salt
- 1 teaspoon black pepper
- 2 sprigs fresh rosemary
- 2 sprigs fresh thyme
- 2 sprigs fresh parsley, plus more for garnish
- 1 cup heavy cream

DIRECTIONS

- Add the butter to a large pot over medium heat. Once the butter is melted, add the onions and celery and cook until tender, about 10 minutes. Add the garlic and cook for 1 minute, then stir in the flour. Add the chicken stock, tomato juice, tomatoes, salt, and pepper. Tie the rosemary, thyme, and parsley together with kitchen twine and add to the pot. Reduce heat and simmer for 30 minutes, stirring occasionally. Remove from heat, discard the herbs, and let cool slightly.

- Working in batches, ladle the bisque into a food processor and process until smooth.

- Stir in the heavy cream and place the pot back over medium heat until hot. Serve hot, garnished with chopped parsley.

TOOLS OF THE TRADE

Immersion Blender: the perfect little tool to quickly and easily blend, puree, and emulsify soups, sauces, smoothies, and dressings.

BY STEVEN BAKER

FLAVORED BUTTER, 3 WAYS

The food processor is perfect for making flavored butter.
From sweet to savory and everything in between, the possibilities are endless.

① HONEY BOURBON BUTTER INGREDIENTS	② SWEET CINNAMON BUTTER INGREDIENTS	③ HERB BUTTER INGREDIENTS
• 1/2 cup salted butter, room temperature	• 1/2 cup salted butter, room temperature	• 1/2 cup salted butter, room temperature
• 2 tablespoons honey	• 2 tablespoons light brown sugar	• 1/2 teaspoon fresh dill
• 1/2 tablespoon bourbon	• 1/2 teaspoon ground cinnamon	• 1/2 teaspoon fresh chives
		• 1/2 teaspoon fresh parsley
		• 1/2 tablespoon lemon juice

DIRECTIONS

Place the ingredients in the food processor and process until combined.

CAST IRON SKILLET

Every kitchen needs a cast iron skillet. They are heavy duty, versatile, inexpensive, virtually indestructible, and come in a wide variety of shapes and sizes. For the purpose of the recipes in this book, I used a 12-inch skillet.

My cast iron skillet actually holds a lot sentimental value because it was my grandparents. A cast iron skillet is so heavy duty that it will last generations if properly cared for. I love cooking in something that my grandparents' used to cook in; it makes meals taste extra special.

The best part about a cast iron skillet is the more you use it, the more seasoned and nonstick it becomes. Every time you cook in the skillet, you're developing another layer of seasoned nonstick coating.

Like a Dutch oven, cast iron skillets are extremely versatile. Use it on the stovetop, in the oven, even over fire. They can be used for everything from fried chicken to desserts to one-pan-meals.

They also hold heat amazingly well, making them perfect for high-heat cooking like searing meat. Once it's hot, it stays hot. The higher the heat, the better the browning, the better the browning, the better the flavor. Since they hold and maintain heat so well, I like to serve food straight from the pan. The food is still warm when folks go back for seconds!

A cast iron skillet is the perfect addition to any kitchen and it's the pan you never knew you needed. You'll find yourself using this pan all the time to make delicious-tasting meals.

CLEANING A CAST IRON SKILLET

When it comes to cleaning a cast iron skillet, there are a lot of dos and don'ts. So much so that it might scare people off from using them. It's actually very easy and doesn't require a lot of extra time.

1. Immediately after use, hand-wash the skillet in hot water and a small amount of mild soap. Scrape off any stuck-on food with a non-abrasive brush or pan scraper. Do not put the skillet in the dishwasher or soak in water.
   For a hard to clean pan, pour 1 cup of water into the skillet and simmer for 5 minutes, then scrape off the stuck-on bits with a wooden spatula.

2. Dry the skillet thoroughly to prevent rusting.

RE-SEASONING A CAST IRON SKILLET

If your cast iron skillet has rust spots or is dull and not as nonstick as it used to be, no worries, because re-seasoning is simple and effortless. In no time, your worn-out skillet will look glossy and new again.

1. Clean the skillet with hot soapy water.

2. Apply a thin layer of vegetable or canola oil all over the pan, including the handle, with a paper towel.

3. Bake in the oven upside down at 450 degrees for 1 hour.

4. Turn the oven off leaving the skillet in to cool completely.

ROAST CHICKEN

SERVINGS: 4

There's something so elegant about a roast chicken. Tender and juicy meat that's infused with amazing flavor from vegetables and herbs. This simple and easy one-pan meal will wow any guest.

INGREDIENTS

- 1-1/2 - 2lbs red potatoes, halved
- 1 medium onion, cut into chunks
- Salt
- Black pepper
- Olive oil

- 4–5lb whole chicken
- 1 whole head garlic, cut in half crosswise
- 1 lemon, quartered
- Several sprigs fresh rosemary
- Several sprigs fresh thyme
- Several fresh sage leaves

DIRECTIONS

- Preheat the oven to 425 degrees.
- Place the potatoes and onions in the bottom of a 12-inch cast iron skillet, then season with salt and black pepper and toss with about 1 tablespoon of olive oil.
- Remove the giblets from the cavity of the chicken and pat the chicken dry with a paper towel. Add salt and pepper liberally to the cavity. Stuff the cavity with the garlic, lemon, rosemary, thyme, and sage and tie the legs of the chicken together with kitchen twine. Brush the chicken with olive oil and sprinkle liberally with salt and pepper.
- Place the chicken breast side up on top of the potatoes. Place the skillet in the oven and cook for approximately 1-1/2 hours until the internal temperature reads 165 degrees. Remove the skillet from the oven, then remove and discard the vegetables and herbs in the cavity. Cover the chicken with aluminum foil and rest for 10-15 minutes before carving.

TOOLS OF THE TRADE

Kitchen Knives: a good set of knives is the most important tool in your kitchen. A well-made, sharp knife will replace a wide array of gadgets that only serve one purpose. A good kitchen knife should be made of good quality material, such as stainless or carbon steel, which ensures longer sharpness.

3 fundamental knives that every kitchen should have:

1. **Chef's Knife:** chopping, dicing, and slicing
2. **Serrated Knife:** cutting vegetables and bread
3. **Paring Knife:** small size for countless jobs

BLACKBERRY COBBLER

SERVINGS: 6-8

This sweet and tangy dessert is perfect with a heaping spoonful of vanilla ice cream on a warm summer night

INGREDIENTS

- 4 cups fresh blackberries
- Zest and juice from 1 lemon
- 1 cup sugar, divided, plus more for topping
- 2 tablespoons cornstarch
- 1-1/2 cups all-purpose flour
- 1-1/2 teaspoons baking powder
- 1/4 teaspoon salt
- 6 tablespoons unsalted butter, cubed
- 1/2 cup buttermilk

DIRECTIONS

- Preheat the oven to 350 degrees.
- Toss together the blackberries, lemon zest, and juice, 1/2 cup sugar, and cornstarch in a 12-inch cast iron skillet.
- In a medium-sized bowl, whisk together the flour, 1/2 cup sugar, baking powder, and salt. Add the butter and cut in with a pastry cutter or 2 forks until the butter is the size of peas. Stir in the buttermilk until the dough is formed. Spread the dough over the top of the blackberries and sprinkle with sugar.
- Bake for 45-55 minutes until bubbly and the crust is golden brown. Serve hot with vanilla ice cream.

TOOLS OF THE TRADE

Pastry Cutter: Easily cut fats like butter and shortening into flour to make dough.

BLONDIE WITH MAPLE CARAMEL DRIZZLE

SERVINGS: 8-10

Blondies are like a giant chocolate chip cookie on steroids.
The rich, sweet, maple caramel drizzle sends this thing into flavor heaven!

INGREDIENTS

Cookie:

- 2 cups all-purpose flour
- 1 teaspoon baking powder
- 1/2 teaspoon salt
- 1-1/2 cups light brown sugar
- 12 tablespoons unsalted butter, melted
- 2 eggs, beaten
- 2 teaspoons vanilla extract
- 1 cup chocolate chips

Maple Caramel Drizzle:

- 3/4 cup sugar
- 1/3 cup water
- 3/4 cup heavy cream
- 2 tablespoons unsalted butter
- 1/2 teaspoon salt
- 2 teaspoons maple extract

DIRECTIONS

- Preheat the oven to 350 degrees. Grease the bottom and sides of a 10 or 12-inch cast iron skillet.

- In a medium-sized bowl, stir together the flour, baking powder, and salt until combined and set aside.

- In a large bowl, stir together the brown sugar and melted butter until combined. Mix in the eggs and vanilla extract. Stir in the flour mixture until well incorporated. Fold in the chocolate chips.

- Pour the batter into the skillet and bake for 25-30 minutes until golden brown and the edges are crisp.

- For the maple caramel drizzle: place the sugar in the bottom of a medium saucepan and pour in the water. Stir gently to moisten the sugar. Place pan over high heat and leave undisturbed until mixture comes to a rolling boil. Continue to let mixture boil rapidly, undisturbed for 3-4 minutes until mixture starts to caramelize. When you start to see color in the pan, gently swirl the pan in a circular motion, do not stir, so mixture caramelizes evenly. When the mixture turns an amber-brown color, remove pan from heat and slowly whisk in heavy cream. Reduce heat to medium and place the pan back on heat. Continue to whisk until sugar is no longer hard, approx. 1-2 minutes. Whisk in butter, salt, and maple extract and remove from heat.

- Spoon the drizzle over the top of the blondie and serve warm with vanilla ice cream.

VODKA SAUCE

MAKES: 4 Cups

An amazing hearty pasta sauce that's perfect for canning to stock up your pantry. This sauce is bursting with flavor along with silky, rich creaminess that will be your new go-to pasta sauce.

INGREDIENTS

- 1/4 cup olive oil
- 2 medium onions, chopped
- 2 teaspoons fresh thyme, chopped
- 2 teaspoons dried oregano
- 1/4 teaspoon red pepper flakes
- 6 garlic cloves, minced

- 1 cup vodka
- (2) 28oz cans whole peeled tomatoes, crushed with your hands
- 2 teaspoon salt
- 1 teaspoon black pepper
- 1/2 cup heavy cream

DIRECTIONS

- Preheat the oven to 375 degrees.

- Add the olive oil to a cast iron skillet over medium heat. Once the oil is hot, add in the onions, thyme, oregano, and red pepper flakes and cook until the onions are soft and translucent, about 5 minutes. Add in the garlic and cook for 1 minute. Stir in the vodka and cook until the vodka is slightly reduced. Stir in the tomatoes, salt, and black pepper. Cover the skillet and place in the oven and cook for 1-1/2 hours.

- Pour the sauce into a food processor or blender and blend until the sauce is smooth. Return the sauce to the skillet and place over low heat. Stir in the heavy cream and simmer until the sauce is heated through. Serve hot tossed with pasta and topped with fresh basil.

COUNTRY-STYLE STEAK

SERVINGS: 4

Country-style steak is country cookin' at its finest! Fork tender cube steak slathered with mouth-watering gravy is a true classic Southern meal. Goes perfect with mashed potatoes or rice.

INGREDIENTS

- 1/2 cup vegetable oil
- 1-1/4 cup all-purpose flour, divided
- Salt
- Black Pepper
- 1/2 teaspoon onion powder
- 1lb cube steak
- 3 cups beef stock
- 2 garlic cloves, minced
- 1 large onion, sliced

DIRECTIONS

- Preheat the oven to 300 degrees.
- Pour the vegetable oil into a cast iron skillet over medium-high heat.
- Add 1 cup of flour, 1/2 tablespoon salt, 1 teaspoon pepper, and the onion powder to a shallow bowl. Dredge the cube steak in the flour mixture, coating each side shaking off any excess.
- Fry the steak in batches for 5 minutes on each side until browned. When done, remove the steaks from the pan and set aside.
- Add 1/4 cup flour and a pinch of salt and pepper to the hot pan and whisk constantly for 1 minute or until the flour turns dark brown, then slowly whisk in the beef stock. Add the steak back into the pan along with the garlic and onions. Cover the pan and bake for 2 hours. Serve hot.

CHICKEN POT PIE

TOOLS OF THE TRADE

Rolling Pin: Easily shape and flatten dough.

SERVINGS: 8

This classic, one-pan meal is the epitome of comfort food. The creamy chicken filling topped with a golden, flakey crust makes for the perfect supper any night of the week.

INGREDIENTS

- 3 chicken breasts, bone in and skin on
- Olive oil
- Salt
- Black pepper
- 1/2 cup unsalted butter
- 1 medium onion, diced
- 1 cup carrots, chopped
- 1/2 cup celery, chopped
- 1 teaspoon fresh thyme, finely chopped
- 3 garlic cloves, minced
- 1/2 cup all-purpose flour
- 1 cup whole milk
- 2 cups chicken stock
- 1 cup potatoes, cut into small cubes
- 1/2 cup frozen peas
- 1/2 teaspoon celery seed
- 1 unbaked pie crust (pg 36)
- 1 egg

DIRECTIONS

- Preheat the oven to 375 degrees. Drizzle the chicken breasts with olive oil, then sprinkle with salt and pepper to taste. Place the chicken on a sheet pan and bake for 45 minutes. Remove from the oven and allow the chicken to cool, then debone and remove the skin and cut into small cubes. Set aside.

- Turn the oven up to 425 degrees.

- Add the butter to a cast iron skillet over medium heat. Once the butter is melted, add the onions, carrots, celery, and thyme and cook for 5 minutes until the onions are soft and translucent. Add the garlic and cook for 1 minute. Whisk in the flour until it clumps up with the vegetables, then slowly whisk in the milk. Stir in the chicken stock and simmer until slightly thickened, about 5 minutes. Remove the skillet from the heat and stir in the potatoes, peas, celery seed, 1 teaspoon salt, 1 teaspoon black pepper, and cooked chicken.

- Roll out the pie crust dough and drape over the top of the skillet. Cut 4 small slits to vent the filling.

- In a small bowl, whisk together the egg and 1 tablespoon of water. Brush the top of the crust with the egg wash, then sprinkle with salt and pepper.

- Place the skillet in the oven and bake for 25 minutes until the crust is golden brown and the filling is bubbly.

CORNBREAD CAKE

SERVINGS: 18-20

While this delectable and moist cake is called cornbread cake, it's not actually cornbread because it doesn't include cornmeal as an ingredient. It just resembles cornbread, hence the name. When I was a kid, my mom would make this and box it up to take on long car rides. It was the perfect snack and it packs up and travel nicely!

INGREDIENTS

- 1-1/2 cups self-rising flour
- 1 cup sugar
- 1 cup light brown sugar
- 1 cup vegetable oil
- 1 teaspoon vanilla extract
- 4 eggs, beaten
- 1 cup pecans, chopped
- Confectioners' sugar

DIRECTIONS

- Place a 12-inch cast iron skillet in the oven and preheat at 350 degrees.

- In a large bowl, stir together the flour, sugar, and brown sugar until combined. Mix in the vegetable oil and vanilla extract until combined. Mix in the eggs and pecans until well incorporated.

- Remove the skillet from the oven and pour in the batter. Place the skillet back in the oven and bake for 30-35 minutes until the center is firm. Remove the skillet from the oven and dust the cake with confectioners' sugar while still hot.

CRAB CAKES WITH SPICY AIOLI

MAKES: 6 Crab Cakes

There's just no better seafood dish than crab cakes! Fresh lump crab meat mixed with just the right amount of other amazing flavors, then fried to perfection is one of my all-time favorite meals.

INGREDIENTS

Crab Cakes:

- 3 tablespoons mayonnaise
- 2 teaspoons Dijon mustard
- 1 teaspoon Worcestershire sauce
- 1 teaspoon lemon juice
- 1/2 teaspoon salt
- 1/4 teaspoon black pepper
- 1 teaspoon Old Bay seasoning
- 1/2 teaspoon garlic powder
- pinch of cayenne pepper
- 2 egg yolks
- 1lb lump crab meat, drained and picked of any shells
- 1/4 cup onions, diced
- 1/4 cup celery, diced
- 1 tablespoon parsley, chopped
- 3/4 cup panko bread crumbs
- 1/4 cup all-purpose flour
- 1/2 cup peanut oil

Spicy Aioli:

- 1 cup mayonnaise
- 1 jalapeño pepper, diced (seeded for less heat)
- 1 teaspoon paprika
- 1/2 teaspoon cayenne pepper
- 2 garlic cloves
- 1/2 teaspoon salt
- 1/2 teaspoon black pepper
- Zest and juice of 1 lime

DIRECTIONS

- In a large bowl, stir together the mayonnaise, Dijon mustard, Worcestershire sauce, lemon juice, salt, black pepper, Old Bay seasoning, garlic powder, cayenne pepper, and egg yolks until combined. Fold in the crab meat, onions, celery, and parsley. Add the panko bread crumbs and flour to a shallow bowl and stir to combine. Take a 1/2 cup portion of the crab meat mixture and shape into a cake. With the cake in the palm of your hand, press the bread crumb mixture onto the crab cake, then repeat for the other side. Repeat to make 5 more cakes. Place the crab cakes in the refrigerator to firm up for at least 30 minutes. Add the peanut oil to a cast iron skillet over medium heat. Once the oil is hot, cook the crab cakes in batches 4-5 minutes on each side until golden brown. Serve warm with spicy aioli.

- For the Aioli, add all ingredients to the bowl of a food processor and process until combined.

OLD-FASHIONED APPLE JACKS

MAKES: 8 Pies

Old-fashioned fried apple pies are that packed with a tender sweet apple filling then enfolded in a lightly fried dough...Southern dessert at its best!

INGREDIENTS

- 4 cups all-purpose flour
- 1 tablespoon baking powder
- 1 teaspoon baking soda
- 1/4 teaspoon salt
- 1 tablespoon shortening
- 1-1/2 cups water
- 3 cups diced Granny Smith apples (about 4 apples), diced
- 3/4 cups sugar, plus more for topping
- 1 teaspoon ground cinnamon, plus more for topping
- 1/4 teaspoon ground ginger
- 1/4 teaspoon nutmeg
- Juice from 1 lemon
- 1 cup vegetable oil

DIRECTIONS

- In a large bowl, combine the flour, baking powder, baking soda, salt, shortening, and water until the dough just comes together. Dump the dough out onto a floured surface and knead the dough into a disc. Wrap the dough in plastic wrap and refrigerate for 1 hour.

- In a medium-sized bowl, stir together the apples, sugar, cinnamon, ginger, nutmeg, and lemon juice. Add the apple mixture to a medium sauce pan over medium heat. Cook for 15-20 minutes, stirring occasionally until the apples become softened and the liquid thickens. Set aside to cool completely.

- Place the dough onto a floured surface and roll out thinly. Cut the dough into quarters, then cut each quarter in half yielding 8 pieces of dough. Spoon about 1 tablespoon of the apple mixture in the center of each dough piece, then fold the dough over and crimp the edge with a fork.

- Add the vegetable oil to a cast iron skillet over medium heat. Working in batches, fry the pies 3-4 minutes each side until golden brown. Remove from the oil and immediately sprinkle with cinnamon and sugar.

SKILLET GREEN BEANS

SERVINGS: 6-8

This delicious and effortless side dish goes great with any meal.

INGREDIENTS

- 2lbs fresh green beans, trimmed
- 5 strips bacon
- 1 tablespoon unsalted butter
- 3 garlic cloves, minced
- Salt
- Black pepper
- Zest and juice of 1 lemon

DIRECTIONS

- Bring a large pot of water to a boil and add in the green beans. Cook for 2 minutes, then plunge the green beans in a large bowl of ice water to stop the cooking. Place the green beans on a paper towel to dry.

- Add the bacon to a cast iron skillet over medium heat and cook until browned. Remove the bacon, roughly chop, and set aside.

- Add the butter to the skillet. When the butter is melted, toss in the green beans, garlic, pinch of salt and black pepper, and lemon zest. Cook for 1-2 minutes until beans are slightly browned, tossing occasionally. Remove from the skillet and toss with lemon juice and bacon.

GRANDMAMA'S SKILLET POTATOES

SERVINGS: 4

As a kid, I would love to watch my grandmama cook and this was one of my absolute favorite things she made. I would request these tender, salty potatoes all the time.

INGREDIENTS

- 1/2 cup vegetable oil
- 2-1/2 - 3lbs russet potatoes, washed, peeled, and diced into 1/2-inch pieces
- 1/4 cup all-purpose flour
- Salt & black pepper to taste

DIRECTIONS

- Add the vegetable oil to a cast iron skillet over medium-high heat.
- In a large bowl, toss the potatoes, flour, salt, and pepper together. Once the oil is hot, add the potatoes to the pan and cook for 15 minutes until tender, stirring occasionally. Remove the potatoes from the skillet and serve warm.

ROASTED TILAPIA WITH LEMON CREAM SAUCE

SERVINGS: 4

This budget-friendly and easy dish is a weeknight dinner dream. It's easy to prepare, cooks fast, and has an amazing creamy, vibrant flavor.

INGREDIENTS

- 4 tilapia fillets
- Salt
- Black Pepper
- Olive oil
- 2 shallots, thinly sliced
- 2 garlic cloves, minced
- 1/2 cup white wine
- Juice from 2 lemons
- 4 tablespoons unsalted butter, melted
- 1/4 cup heavy cream
- Fresh parsley, chopped

DIRECTIONS

- Preheat the oven to 400 degrees. Season the tilapia fillets with salt and pepper and set aside.

- Add 1-2 tablespoons of olive oil to a cast iron skillet over medium heat. Once hot, add the shallots and cook until tender, about 5 minutes. Add the garlic and cook for 1 minute. Add the white wine and cook until the wine is reduced by half, about 1 minute. Stir in the lemon juice, melted butter, heavy cream, and 1 teaspoon of pepper. Place the tilapia fillets into the skillet and place the skillet into the oven.

- Bake for 10-12 minutes until the fillets are flakey. Serve hot topped with the pan sauce and parsley.

VEGETARIAN STIR FRY

TOOLS OF THE TRADE

Zester: great for extracting maximum flavor from citrus peels, garlic, and fresh ginger and also grating cheeses.

SERVINGS: 4

*Colorful tender vegetables, stir-fried together in a sweet
and savory sauce served alongside rice or noodles, is the perfect weeknight dinner.*

INGREDIENTS

- 1/2 cup soy sauce
- 1/2 cup vegetable broth
- 1 tablespoon peanut butter
- 1 tablespoon honey
- 1 teaspoon rice vinegar
- 1/2 teaspoon sesame oil
- 1 tablespoon corn starch
- 2 garlic cloves, minced
- 1 teaspoon grated fresh ginger

- Peanut oil
- 3 cups butternut squash, cubed
- 1-1/2 cups broccoli florets
- 1/2 cup onion, sliced
- 1/2 cup zucchini, sliced
- 1/2 cup sugar snap peas
- 1/4 cup carrots, sliced
- 1/2 red bell pepper, sliced
- Green onions for garnish, chopped

DIRECTIONS

- In a medium sized bowl, whisk together the soy sauce, vegetable broth, peanut butter, honey, rice vinegar, sesame oil, corn starch, garlic, and ginger. Set aside.

- Add 2 tablespoons of the peanut oil to a cast iron skillet over medium heat. Once hot, add the butternut squash and cook for 10-12 minutes until browned and tender. Remove the butternut squash from the skillet and set aside.

- Add 2 more tablespoons of peanut oil and the rest of the vegetables to the skillet. Cook for 2-3 minutes until the vegetables just start to brown. Add the butternut squash back to the skillet. Stir in the sauce until heated through, then remove the skillet from the heat. Serve hot over rice topped with green onions.

DUTCH OVEN

When it comes to cookware, you don't get much more versatile, durable, and functional than a Dutch oven. These heavy-duty pots that have been around for hundreds of years have recently skyrocketed in popularity. They can do everything from fry, roast, braise, bake, and slow-cook a wide range of recipes, plus you can use different heat sources to cook with (stovetop, oven, grill).

Dutch ovens are made from cast iron which makes them extremely sturdy and durable. They are so great at cooking because they help with heat retention and distribution, which ensures food cooks evenly. They're also great heat conductors. You can sear meat over high heat on the stovetop, then immediately transfer the pot to the oven for low and slow cooking. Dutch ovens come with an airtight lid that retains moisture in the pot which will elevate flavors in food. Because the lid is air tight, Dutch ovens are perfect for baking bread. The lid seals in moisture inside the pot allowing the build-up of steam which produces air bubbles in the bread, creating a crusty exterior.

All Dutch ovens are cast iron, but Dutch ovens that are finished in an enamel coating have become increasingly popular. The straight cast iron Dutch ovens are the original Dutch ovens and have to be cared for and maintained just like a cast iron skillet. The enamel finished Dutch ovens have an enamel finish over the interior and exterior creating a smooth surface. These are easier to care for, but are generally more expensive. Enamel finished Dutch ovens don't need to be seasoned and are not prone to rusting. Dutch ovens might look like just a smaller stockpot, but they are a world of different. Stockpots are taller and lighter, making them ideal for soups and stews, plus you can only use a stockpot on the stovetop. Dutch ovens are shorter and thicker, maintaining a constant temperature in the pot so food cooks evenly.

Dutch ovens come in a wide variety of shapes and sizes which effects the price. Consider what you'll be using a Dutch oven for to determine the size that's right for you. For the purpose of the recipes in this book, I used a 6-quart Dutch oven.

OLD-FASHIONED BRUNSWICK STEW

MAKES: 6-1/2 Quarts

I was recently asked what was the secret to good Brunswick stew. The special ingredient is to use hens rather than chickens. Because hens are just mature chickens, they have more fat, which means more flavor. My dad will make a huge pot of this in the fall for us to freeze and eat all winter long.

INGREDIENTS

- 1 whole (5-6lb) hen, cut into quarters
- 1/2 head cabbage, cut into quarters
- 1lb dry lima beans
- 1lb potatoes, cubed
- 1lb frozen butter beans
- 1 tablespoon salt
- 1/2 tablespoon black pepper
- 1/2 tablespoon red pepper flakes
- 4 cups tomato juice
- (2) 15oz cans cream style corn

DIRECTIONS

- Add the hen quarters to a large stockpot filled with water and boil for 1 hour. When done, remove the hen reserving the stock. When the hen is cooled, debone and reserve the skin. Set aside.
- Add the cabbage and dry lima beans to a large Dutch oven and fill with water. Bring the pot to a boil, then reduce and simmer for 2 hours, stirring occasionally and adding more water as needed. Add the hen meat and skin, hen stock, potatoes, butter beans, salt, pepper, and red pepper flakes to the Dutch oven. Simmer for 45 minutes to 1 hour stirring occasionally until thickened. Add in the tomato juice and corn and simmer for 15 minutes stirring constantly. Serve hot.

CHICKEN AND PASTRY

SERVINGS: 4-6

This old-fashioned Southern dish is the perfect lazy, rainy-day meal you'll make again and again.

INGREDIENTS

- 1 (3-4lb) whole chicken
- 1 medium onion, diced
- 2 bay leaves
- Salt
- Black pepper

- 2 cups all-purpose flour
- 1 tablespoon baking powder
- 8 cups chicken stock
- 2 tablespoons cornstarch
- Fresh parsley, roughly chopped

DIRECTIONS

- In a large Dutch oven, add the chicken, onions, bay leaves, 2 teaspoons salt, 1 teaspoon pepper, and 4 quarts of water. Bring the pot to a boil, partially cover with the lid, and cook for 45 minutes until the meat begins to fall off the bone. Remove the chicken and set aside to cool, reserving the stock. Once cooled, debone the chicken and add back to the pot.

- Sift together the flour, baking powder, 1 teaspoon salt, and 1/2 teaspoon black pepper into a large bowl. Add 3/4 cup ice water and stir until the dough comes together. Dump out the dough onto a floured surface and knead until the ball of dough forms. Roll the dough out to about 1/4-inch thick and cut into slices.

- Add the extra 8 cups of chicken stock to the pot and bring to a boil. Add the slices of pastry to the pot without stirring. Cook for about 5 minutes until the pastry floats to the top.

- In a small bowl, whisk together the cornstarch and 1 cup of the chicken stock from the pot. Add back to the pot and stir to thicken the stock. Serve hot topped with parsley.

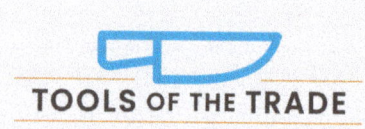

TOOLS OF THE TRADE

Durable Cookware: Good cookware really depends on your preference and budget. They come in all sorts of sizes and types of material they're made with (stainless steel, copper, etc). Cookware can get very expensive and each different material can cook differently.

Basic cookware every kitchen should have (regardless of material):
- Large stock pot
- 12in non-stick skillet
- 2, 1.5, & 1qt sauce pans
- 10in sauté pan
- Roaster

OLD-FASHIONED COLLARD GREENS

SERVINGS: 6-8

This classic Southern staple is best eaten in the fall when it's a bit chilly, because the cool weather makes them a touch sweeter. These collards are slow-cooked with a fat ham hock for that perfect flavor just like grandma used to make!

INGREDIENTS

- 1 large ham hock (1/2 – 1lb)
- 1/4 cup bacon grease
- 1 medium onion, diced
- 4-5 garlic cloves, minced
- 1/2 teaspoon salt
- 1-1/2 teaspoons black pepper
- 1/2 teaspoon red pepper flakes
- 2 tablespoons apple cider vinegar
- 2lbs collard greens, washed and stems removed

DIRECTIONS

- In a large Dutch oven or stockpot, add 12 cups water, the ham hock, bacon grease, onions, garlic, salt, pepper, red pepper flakes, and vinegar and bring to a boil. Add the collards, several leaves at a time, until all the collards are in the pot. The collards will begin to wilt as they are put into the boiling water. Reduce the heat to low and simmer uncovered for 2 hours.

- Removed the collards with a slotted spoon and chop to desired consistency. Take the meat off of the ham hock and add to the collards.

BLACKBERRY JAM

MAKES: 2-1/2 Pints

A sweet jam with just the right tartness that takes only a few ingredients is something you'll be enjoying all year long.

INGREDIENTS

- 5 cups fresh blackberries
- 5 cups sugar
- Zest from 1 lemon
- Juice from 2 lemons

DIRECTIONS

- Add the blackberries to a large Dutch oven or stock pot and mash with a potato masher. Add the sugar and lemon zest and juice and bring to a boil, stirring constantly. Cook, stirring constantly until the temperature of the jam reads 220F with a candy thermometer, 5-10 minutes.

- Remove the pot from the heat. To test the doneness of the jam, place a plate in the freezer until very cold. Add about 1 teaspoon of the jam to the plate and place back in the freezer for 1-2 minutes. Remove the plate and run your finger through the middle of the jam. If the jam does not run, then it's done. If the jam needs to cook more, return the pot to the heat and test again in 1-2 minutes. Be careful not to overcook the jam.

- Strain half of the jam through a sieve to remove some of the seeds. Allow the jam to cool at room temperature and refrigerate for up to 2 weeks or can the jam in jars to keep longer.

CORN CHOWDER

SERVINGS: 6

Nothing beats the taste of fresh corn. The corn cobs help make the most delicious flavorful stock ever. This creamy, sweet soup is prefect for summer or winter.

INGREDIENTS

- 8-10 ears corn, husks and silks removed
- 4 cups chicken stock
- 2 cups whole milk
- 4 strips bacon, chopped
- 2 tablespoons unsalted butter
- 1 medium onion, diced
- 2 whole carrots, chopped
- 2 celery stalks, chopped
- 1 teaspoon fresh thyme, chopped
- 2 garlic cloves, minced
- 1 cup heavy cream
- 1lb potatoes, cubed
- 1 tablespoon salt
- 1/2 tablespoon black pepper
- Fresh chives, chopped

DIRECTIONS

- Over a large bowl, cut the corn kernels off the cob, reserving the cobs for the stock. Set aside.

- To make the stock, add the corn cobs, chicken stock, and milk to a stockpot. Bring to a boil, then reduce the heat and simmer for 20 minutes stirring occasionally. Discard the cobs when done.

- Place a Dutch oven over medium heat. Once hot, add the bacon and cook until browned. Remove the bacon with a slotted spoon and set aside. Add the butter, onions, carrots, celery, and thyme to the Dutch oven and cook until tender, about 5 minutes. Add the garlic and cook for 1 minute. Stir in the reserved stock, heavy cream, potatoes, salt, pepper, and corn kernels. Bring to a boil, then reduce the heat and simmer for 30 minutes, stirring occasionally. Serve hot, topped with bacon and chives.

BY STEVEN BAKER

CLASSIC STEAMED MUSSELS

SERVINGS: 2

An elegant, flavorful dish made with a rich wine sauce that's so easy to make you won't believe it.

INGREDIENTS

- 2 tablespoons olive oil
- 1 medium shallot, diced
- 4 garlic cloves, minced
- 1 teaspoon fresh thyme, chopped
- 3 tablespoons unsalted butter
- 2lbs fresh mussels, cleaned

- 1 cup dry white wine, such as sauvignon blanc
- 1/2 cup heavy cream
- 1/2 teaspoon salt
- 1/2 teaspoon black pepper
- Zest and juice of 1 lemon
- Fresh parsley, roughly chopped

DIRECTIONS

- Add the olive oil to a Dutch oven over medium heat. Once hot, add the shallots, garlic, and thyme and cook for 1 minute. Add the butter. Once the butter is melted, add the mussels and toss in the butter to coat. Stir in the white wine, heavy cream, salt, pepper, and lemon zest and juice. Place the lid on the Dutch oven and cook for 10 minutes until the mussels are opened and cooked through.

- Discard any mussels that did not open during cooking. Serve hot in bowls topped with cooking juice and parsley.

STRAWBERRY PRESERVES

TOOLS OF THE TRADE

Candy Thermometer: easily measure the temperature of boiling sugar, oil, sauces, and syrups.

MAKES: 3-1/2 Pints

My absolute favorite thing to make in the spring is strawberry preserves.
The fresh-picked strawberries have a tart, sweetness that just cannot be matched.
I make a big batch of preserves, can them, and enjoy this treat all year long.

INGREDIENTS

- 4lbs fresh strawberries, hulled and quartered
- 2 cups sugar
- 1 granny smith apple, peeled and diced
- 1/3 cup freshly squeezed lemon juice

DIRECTIONS

- Add all the ingredients to a Dutch oven over medium heat. Cook stirring often until the mixture begins to boil. Cook for 25-30 minutes, stirring often until the temperature reads 215 degrees on a candy thermometer. Remove from heat and allow to cool to room temperature.

- To can the preserves, bring a large stockpot with a canning rack in the bottom to a boil. Fill sterilized canning jars with the preserves so that they have 1/4 inch of space from the top of the jar. Wipe the mouths of the jars clean of any residue and place the lid on the jars hand tight. Lower the jars onto the canning rack in the boiling water, making sure the jars are covered with water. Boil for 15 minutes, then remove the jars from the pot and set on a cooling rack. Let the jars cool to room temperature until they are sealed (you'll hear them pop and the lid center will have no give) and tighten the lids. Store at room temperature.

DUCK STEW

SERVINGS: 6

Duck stew is the perfect supper on a cold night. Slow-cooking is the secret to turning this lean game into a hearty, delicious meal.

INGREDIENTS

- 1-1/2 lbs duck breast, cut into chunks
- 1/4 cup all-purpose flour
- 2 tablespoons canola oil
- 3 tablespoons unsalted butter
- 1 medium onion, diced
- 1 cup baby carrots
- 1-1/2 teaspoons fresh thyme, chopped
- 4 garlic cloves, minced
- 1 cup red wine
- 10 cups beef stock
- 1 tablespoon rosemary, chopped
- 1 teaspoon salt
- 1 teaspoon black pepper
- 2 bay leaves
- 2 cups red potatoes, halved
- 2 tablespoons tomato paste
- 1-1/2 cups white rice
- Fresh parsley, chopped

DIRECTIONS

- Preheat the oven to 325 degrees.

- Toss the duck and flour together to coat, then knock off any excess flour.

- Add the canola oil to a Dutch oven over medium-high heat. Once the oil is hot, add the duck to the Dutch oven and cook until browned, about 3-5 minutes. Remove the duck with a slotted spoon and set aside.

- Reduce the heat to medium and add the butter to the Dutch oven. Once melted, add the onions, carrots, and thyme and cook until tender, about 5 minutes. Add the garlic and cook for 1 minute. Add the wine and let cook until slightly reduced, about 5 minutes. Add the beef stock, rosemary, salt, pepper, bay leaves, and duck. Place the lid on the Dutch oven, place in the oven, and cook for 3 hours.

- Place the Dutch oven back on the stove and remove the lid. Add the potatoes and tomato paste and bring the pot to a boil. Add in the rice, place the lid back on, reduce the heat, and simmer for 20 minutes. Serve hot, garnished with parsley.

JAMBALAYA

SERVINGS: 6-8

Jambalaya is the ultimate one-pot meal. This Cajun classic is packed full of flavorful meats and vegetables that will quickly become a family favorite.

INGREDIENTS

- Olive Oil
- 1lb andouille sausage, sliced
- 2 boneless chicken breasts, cubed
- Salt
- Black pepper
- 1 medium onion, diced
- 2 celery stalks, chopped
- 2 red bell peppers, chopped
- 1 jalapeño pepper, chopped (seeded for less heat)
- 1 teaspoon fresh thyme, chopped
- 4 garlic cloves, minced
- 14oz can whole peeled tomatoes, cores removed and crushed with your hands
- 4 cups chicken stock
- 2 teaspoons Creole seasoning
- 2 bay leaves
- 1-1/2 cups white rice
- 1lb shrimp, peeled and deveined
- 1 cup okra (thawed if using frozen)
- Juice from 1 lemon
- Fresh parsley for garnish

DIRECTIONS

- Add 2 tablespoons of olive oil to a Dutch oven over medium heat. Once the oil is hot, add the andouille sausage and cook until browned, 4-5 minutes. Remove with a slotted spoon and set aside. Season the chicken with salt and black pepper, then add to the pot and cook until browned, 5 minutes. Remove with a slotted spoon and set aside.

- Add 1 tablespoon of olive oil to the pot, then add in the onions, celery, red bell pepper, jalapeño pepper, 1/2 teaspoon black pepper, and thyme and cook until the onions are soft and translucent, about 5 minutes. Add the garlic and cook for 1 minute. Add in the tomatoes, chicken stock, Creole seasoning, bay leaves, white rice, andouille sausage, and chicken, then adjust the heat to high and bring to a boil. Reduce the heat to low, place the lid on, and simmer for 20 minutes.

- Stir in the shrimp and okra, place the lid back on, and let cook for 5 minutes. Remove from the heat, stir in the lemon juice, and discard the bay leaves. Serve hot garnished with parsley.

KITCHEN CLAMBAKE

SERVINGS: 6-8

One big delicious meal in one big pot. This seafood feast is perfect for get-togethers and, best of all, doesn't require hours of preparation.

INGREDIENTS

- 3 dozen littleneck clams
- 2lbs mussels
- 6 tablespoons unsalted butter
- 2 shallots, diced
- 1 teaspoon fresh thyme, chopped
- 4 garlic cloves, minced
- 1lb red potatoes, halved
- 4 ears corn, cut in half
- 1-1/2 cups white wine
- Juice from 1 lemon
- 1 teaspoon salt
- 1 teaspoon black pepper
- 1 teaspoon Old Bay seasoning
- 1lb jumbo shrimp, in the shell

DIRECTIONS

- To clean the clams: soak the clams in a large bowl of salted cold water for 20 minutes. Scrub each clam with a brush or sponge to remove any debris from the shell. Discard any clam that is open. Set aside.

- To clean the mussels: soak the mussels in cold water for 20 minutes. Remove the beards from each mussel and scrub with a brush or sponge under cold water to remove any debris. Discard any mussel that is open. Set aside.

- Add the butter to a large Dutch oven over medium heat. Once the butter is melted, add in the shallots and thyme and cook for 5 minutes until the shallots are soft and translucent. Add in the garlic, potatoes, and corn and cook for 1 minute. Stir in the white wine, lemon juice, salt, pepper, and Old Bay seasoning. Add in the clams and mussels. Place the lid on and cook for 10 minutes.

- Add in the shrimp, place the lid back on, and cook for 5 minutes until the shrimp are opaque and the clams and mussels have opened. Serve warm with cooking broth.

TURKEY BREAST WITH PAN GRAVY

SERVINGS: 4-6

Thanksgiving made easy with this simple, tender, and juicy holiday staple.

INGREDIENTS

- 5-6lb turkey breast
- Salt
- Black pepper
- 3 tablespoons olive oil
- 1 small onion, chopped
- 1 carrot, chopped
- 1 celery stalk, chopped
- 6 garlic cloves, minced
- Several fresh sprigs of rosemary, thyme, and sage
- 1 lemon
- 1/4 cup all-purpose flour
- 4 cups chicken stock

DIRECTIONS

- Preheat the oven to 300 degrees. Pat the turkey breast dry with paper towels, then sprinkle liberally with salt and black pepper.

- Add the olive oil to the Dutch oven over medium heat. Once the oil is hot, place the turkey in the pot breast side down. Add the onions, carrots, and celery and cook for 10 minutes. Flip the turkey breast to skin side up, then add in the garlic, herbs, and squeeze the lemon juice into the pot, then add in the lemons. Place the lid on the Dutch oven and place in the oven. Cook for 1-1/2 - 2 hours until the internal temperature of the turkey breast reads 165 degrees. Remove the turkey breast from the Dutch oven and wrap in aluminum foil to rest. Rest for 15 minutes before carving.

- Remove the liquid pan drippings from the pot reserving 1/4 cup. Add the reserved pan drippings and the cooked vegetables back to the Dutch oven over medium heat. Once hot, whisk in the flour and continue to whisk for 30 seconds until the flour clumps up. Slowly whisk in the chicken stock. Add salt and black pepper to taste. Simmer for 10-15 minutes until the gravy thickens, then pour the gravy through a sieve to separate the liquid.

SUMMER SUCCOTASH

SERVINGS: 6-7

I love to make this classic Southern dish with fresh-picked vegetables straight from my dad's garden. All the different ingredients marry amazingly well together and it pairs great with any entrée.

INGREDIENTS

- 2 tablespoons olive oil
- 4 cups fresh corn kernels (about 8 ears) (thawed if using frozen)
- 1/2 cup red onion, chopped
- 1 red bell pepper, chopped
- 1 jalapeño pepper, minced (seeded for less heat)
- 4-5 garlic cloves, minced
- 2 cups fresh butter beans (thawed if using frozen)
- 2 teaspoons salt
- 1 teaspoon black pepper
- 2 tablespoons unsalted butter
- 5-6 basil leaves, roughly chopped
- Juice from 1 lemon
- Fresh parsley, roughly chopped

DIRECTIONS

- Add the olive oil to a Dutch oven over medium heat. Once the oil is hot, add the corn and cook stirring occasionally for 4-5 minutes until the corn is tender. Add the onion, bell pepper, and jalapeño pepper and cook for 3 minutes. Add the garlic and cook for 1 minute. Next, add the butter beans, salt, and pepper and cook for 5 minutes until the butter beans are tender. Add the butter and stir until melted.

- Remove the Dutch oven from the heat and stir in basil and lemon juice. Serve warm topped with parsley.

HALF-SHEET PAN

I'm all about multitasking in the kitchen. I love one product that does a whole array of different things. A half-sheet pan is definitely one of the most versatile kitchen tools you can have. Not only are they extremely versatile, but they're also very durable and provide for easy clean up.

Half-sheet pans are most common in your standard household because full sheet pans are too large for the common oven.

With a half-sheet pan, you can do everything from roasting batches of vegetables, to broiling meat, even baking desserts. The shallowness of the pan allows the heat from the oven to fully surround what you're cooking to bring out the full flavor of the ingredients. Recipes can range from quick one-pan meals to easy snacks and everything in between. The thing that I use a half-sheet pan most for is roasting vegetables, which makes the perfect side dish. It's so easy to toss whatever vegetables I have on hand with some oil, roast them, and in less than half an hour I've got tender flavorful roasted vegetables. These little guys are also a baker's best friend. They're perfect for batches of cookies, candy bark, even full cakes.

I have several half-sheet pans and I still don't seem to have enough at my disposal. I not only use them for cooking, but I also use them to prep ingredients and even to serve food from. I also recommend purchasing quarter-sheet pans as well. Quarter-sheet pans do everything half-sheet pan do, only they're smaller which means they're easier to handle and easier to clean.

No matter what type of cooking you plan on doing, this underrated cookware is a must-have for any kitchen.

TURKEY MEATLOAF WITH GARLIC GRAVY

SERVINGS: 6

Forget what you know about meatloaf! You haven't had meatloaf until you've had it served with seasoned-to-perfection garlic gravy. This is a weekly must-have!

INGREDIENTS

Meatloaf:

- 1 tablespoon olive oil
- 1/2 cup onions, chopped
- 1/2 cup portobello mushrooms, chopped
- 1 teaspoon fresh thyme, chopped
- 2 garlic cloves, minced
- 1/4 cup beef stock
- 2 tablespoons Worcestershire sauce
- 1 tablespoon tomato paste
- 2lbs ground turkey
- 1/2 cup Italian bread crumbs
- 2 eggs
- Salt & black pepper
- Fresh parsley, roughly chopped

Garlic Gravy:

- 1/4 cup vegetable oil or bacon grease
- 1 head garlic, cloves smashed
- Several sprigs fresh thyme
- 1/4 cup all-purpose flour
- 4 cups chicken stock
- Salt & black pepper
- 2 tablespoons corn starch

DIRECTIONS

- Preheat the oven to 325 degrees. Line a half-sheet pan with parchment paper.

- Add the olive oil to a medium-sized sauté pan over medium heat. Once hot, add the onions, mushrooms, and thyme and cook for 5 minutes until the onions are tender. Add the garlic and cook for 1 minute. Stir in the beef stock, Worcestershire sauce, and tomato paste. Remove pan from heat and set aside to cool slightly.

- In a large bowl, combine the ground turkey, bread crumbs, eggs, salt and pepper to taste, and onion mixture. Place the mixture on the half-sheet pan and form into a loaf. Bake for 1-1/2 hours until the internal temperature reads 160 degrees.

- For the garlic gravy, heat the oil/grease in a large frying pan over medium heat. Once hot, add the garlic and thyme sprigs and cook for 2 minutes. Add in the flour and whisk for 30 seconds. Add the chicken stock and salt and pepper to taste and simmer for 10 minutes stirring constantly. Strain the gravy through a sieve and add the gravy back to the pan.

- In a small bowl, whisk together the corn starch and 1/2 cup hot water. Add to the gravy and simmer for 2 minutes until the gravy is thickened.

- Slice the meatloaf and top with gravy and parsley.

SHEET-PAN BUTTER CAKE WITH CHOCOLATE ICING

SERVINGS: 36-45

This buttery, moist cake topped with buttercream chocolate frosting is the perfect cake for birthday parties or for just any ol' time. My favorite part about this cake is it's only one layer. No icing multiple layers! Easiest cake ever!

INGREDIENTS

Cake:

- 3 cups cake flour
- 1 tablespoon baking powder
- 1/2 teaspoon baking soda
- 1/4 teaspoon salt
- 1 cup unsalted butter, room temperature
- 1-1/2 cups sugar
- 2 teaspoons vanilla extract
- 4 eggs, room temperature
- 1 cup whole milk

Chocolate Icing:

- 1/2 cup cocoa powder
- 3 cups confectioners' sugar
- 1 cup unsalted butter, room temperature
- 1 teaspoon vanilla extract
- 4oz semi-sweet chocolate, melted and cooled
- Pinch of salt
- 1/4 cup heavy cream

DIRECTIONS

- Preheat the oven to 350 degrees and line a 12x18 half-sheet pan with parchment paper, then spray with cooking spray.

- Sift together the flour, baking powder, baking soda, and salt into a medium-sized bowl and set aside.

- In a stand mixer bowl fitted with the paddle attachment, beat the butter, sugar, and vanilla extract until creamy, about 5 minutes. With the mixer on low, add the eggs one at a time until well incorporated. Slowly add in the flour mixture and milk a little at a time, starting and ending with the flour mixture.

- Pour the batter evenly into the pan and smooth the top with a rubber spatula. Bake for 20-25 minutes until a toothpick comes out clean. Set aside to cool to room temperature.

- For the icing, sift together the cocoa powder and confectioners' sugar and set aside.

- In the bowl of a stand mixer fitted with the whisk attachment, beat the butter until creamed, about 3-4 minutes. Mix in the vanilla, melted chocolate, and salt until well incorporated. With the mixer on low, slowly add in the cocoa powder mixture and heavy cream a little at a time stopping every so often to scrape down the sides of the bowl. Mix on medium speed until smooth and creamy, about 2-3 minutes. Spread the icing evenly on the cake.

SPAGHETTI AND MEATBALLS

SERVINGS: 4-6

Spaghetti is good, but spaghetti and meatballs are out of this world and make for the perfect weeknight dinner. The roasted meatballs are tasty, juicy, and so easy to make. What's not to love about this classic Italian dish!

INGREDIENTS

- 2lbs ground beef
- 1 cup Italian bread crumbs
- 1/2 cup freshly grated Parmesan cheese
- 1 tablespoon garlic powder
- 1/2 tablespoon onion powder
- 1 teaspoon salt
- 1/2 teaspoon black pepper

- 2 tablespoons fresh basil, chopped
- 2 tablespoons fresh parsley, chopped
- 2 eggs
- (2) 24oz jars marinara sauce
- 1lb spaghetti noodles
- Extra Parmesan cheese and parsley for garnish

DIRECTIONS

- Preheat the oven to 400 degrees. Line a half-sheet pan with parchment paper.

- In a large bowl, add the ground beef, bread crumbs, Parmesan cheese, garlic powder, onion powder, salt, pepper, basil, parsley, and eggs and mix together with your hands until combined. Using a 1.5 tablespoon ice cream scoop, scoop out the mixture and roll into balls, then place on the baking sheet. Mixture will yield about 30 meatballs. Bake the meatballs for 30 minutes until browned.

- While the meatballs are cooking, add the marinara sauce to a large pot and simmer over low heat. In a separate pot, cook the spaghetti noodles according to the package directions.

- When the meatballs are done, remove from the oven and add to the marinara sauce. Ladle the meatballs and marinara sauce over spaghetti noodles and top with Parmesan cheese and parsley.

SHEET-PAN PIZZA

SERVINGS: 6

It's not delivery...it's just a simple, tasty pizza that the whole family will love. Cowabunga!

INGREDIENTS

- 1 pizza dough (pg 28), room temperature
- Olive oil
- 1 teaspoon fresh thyme, chopped
- 3/4 - 1 cup pizza sauce
- 2 cups mozzarella cheese, shredded
- 1 cup parmesan cheese, shredded
- pepperoni slices

DIRECTIONS

- Preheat the oven to 450 degrees and lightly grease a half-sheet pan.
- Stretch the dough out to the shape of the pan. Brush the top of the dough with 1-2 tablespoons of olive oil, then sprinkle the thyme over the top. Evenly distribute the pizza sauce over the top leaving 1/2-inch border from the edge. Spread mozzarella cheese, Parmesan cheese, and pepperoni over the top. You can also add any other ingredients that you like as well.
- Place the pan on the bottom rack of the oven. Bake for 15 minutes or until the crust is golden brown.

ROASTED CHICKPEAS

MAKES: 4 Cups

Roasted chickpeas are a great go-to protein snack that can be made with a countless variety of flavors.

INGREDIENTS

- (2) 15.5oz cans chickpeas, drained, rinsed & patted dry
- 1 tablespoon Old Bay seasoning

DIRECTIONS

Preheat the oven to 450 degrees. Toss the chickpeas with the Old Bay seasoning, then transfer them to a half-sheet pan and bake for 25 minutes, tossing occasionally.

ROASTED CHICKEN SALAD

SERVINGS: 4-5

Roasting chicken for a chicken salad provides so much more flavor than boiling it. This recipe will turn the volume way up on any potluck or picnic!

INGREDIENTS

- 3 chicken breasts, bone in and skin on
- Olive oil
- Salt
- Black Pepper
- 3/4 cup red onion, chopped
- 1/2 cup celery, chopped
- 2 tablespoons fresh dill, chopped
- 1 tablespoon fresh tarragon, chopped
- 1 cup mayonnaise
- Juice from 1 lemon

DIRECTIONS

- Preheat the oven to 375 degrees.
- Drizzle the chicken with olive oil and sprinkle with salt and pepper. Place the chicken on a half-sheet pan and bake for 45 minutes or until the internal temperature reads 165 degrees. Remove from the oven and set aside to cool.
- Remove the meat from the bone and discard the skin. Cut the chicken into small bite-sized pieces.
- In a large bowl, toss together the chicken, red onion, celery, dill, tarragon, mayonnaise, lemon juice, 1/2 teaspoon salt, and 1/4 teaspoon pepper. Serve with toast or crackers.

TOOLS OF THE TRADE

Vacuum Sealer: Store meat and vegetables for long periods of time while preserving flavor and texture. Perfect for buying in bulk and meal prep.

PANKO-CRUSTED CHICKEN THIGHS

SERVINGS: 6

This oven baked chicken is flavorful, succulent, and cheap to make.
The tender and juicy chicken topped with the buttery crispy crust makes for the perfect supper.

INGREDIENTS

- 1/2 cup white wine
- Zest and juice of 1 lemon
- 1 egg
- 1-1/2 cups panko bread crumbs
- 2 teaspoons fresh thyme, chopped
- 1 teaspoon salt
- 1/2 teaspoon black pepper
- 6 chicken thighs, bone in and skin on
- 3 tablespoons unsalted butter, melted

DIRECTIONS

- Preheat the oven to 400 degrees.
- In a shallow bowl, whisk together the wine, lemon juice, and egg. In another shallow bowl, combine the panko bread crumbs, thyme, salt, pepper, and lemon zest.
- Dip the chicken in the wine mixture, then dredge in the bread crumbs skin side only. Place the chicken on a half-sheet pan skin side up, then press the remaining bread crumbs on top. Drizzle the melted butter on top of the chicken.
- Bake for 35-40 minutes until the internal temperature reads 170 degrees.

CHICKEN TERIYAKI KABOBS

SERVINGS: 4-5

Were you planning on grilling out but the weather messed that up? No worries with this easy oven-roasted recipe. These kabobs are stacked with juicy marinated chicken and tender vegetables. Perfectly cooked kabobs and you never have to step outside!

INGREDIENTS

- 1 cup teriyaki sauce
- 2 tablespoons olive oil
- 2 tablespoons Worcestershire sauce
- 1 tablespoon brown sugar
- 2 garlic cloves, minced
- 1/2 teaspoon black pepper

- Zest and juice of 1 lemon
- 3 boneless skinless chicken breasts, cut into 1-inch pieces
- 1 red onion, cut into 1-inch pieces
- 2 bell peppers, cut into 1-inch pieces
- 8oz whole mushrooms, stems removed

DIRECTIONS

- In a small bowl, whisk together the teriyaki sauce, olive oil, Worcestershire sauce, brown sugar, garlic, black pepper, and lemon zest and juice. Place the chicken pieces and teriyaki marinade in a zipper-lock bag and refrigerate for 5-6 hours.

- Preheat the oven to 425 degrees and line a half-sheet pan with aluminum foil.

- Alternately place the chicken pieces and vegetables on skewers. If using wood skewers, make sure to soak them in water overnight to prevent burning. Place the skewers in the pan and drizzle the skewers with remaining marinade.

- Cook for 20 minutes, flipping the skewers halfway through. Turn the oven to broil and cook each side until slightly charred.

MERINGUE COOKIES

MAKES: 24 Cookies

Lighter-than-air cookies that are delicate, sweet, and a breeze to make. Great for holidays and parties.

INGREDIENTS

- 4 egg whites, room temperature
- 1/4 teaspoon salt
- 1/4 teaspoon cream of tartar
- 1 cup sugar
- 1 teaspoon vanilla extract

DIRECTIONS

- Preheat the oven to 200 degrees and line 2 half-sheet pans with parchment paper. Add egg whites, salt, and cream of tartar to a stand mixer bowl fitted with the whisk attachment. Beat on medium speed until the egg whites are frothy and soft peaks form, about 1 minute. Turn the mixer to high speed and add the sugar 1 tablespoon at a time until incorporated. Beat for 4-5 minutes until the meringue is the consistency of marshmallow cream and forms stiff peaks. Fold in the vanilla extract with a rubber spatula.

- Spoon the meringue into a piping bag fitted with a large star tip. Pipe 2-inch cookies on the sheet pans leaving an inch between cookies. Bake for 1 hour, then turn off the heat and leave the cookies in the oven for an additional 2 hours.

ROASTED BRUSSELS SPROUTS

SERVES: 6

Brussels Sprouts have a bad reputation but these are not the mushy, soggy, green blobs you thought they were when you were a kid. They're roasted until they're perfectly tender then tossed with just enough balsamic vinegar to accentuate the other flavors. Eating your greens never tasted so good!

INGREDIENTS

- 1-1/2lbs Brussels sprouts, halved
- 1 teaspoon salt
- 1/2 teaspoon black pepper
- 1/4 teaspoon red pepper flakes
- 3 tablespoons olive oil
- 3 tablespoons balsamic vinegar

DIRECTIONS

- Preheat the oven to 400 degrees.
- Toss together the Brussels sprouts, salt, black pepper, red pepper flakes, and olive oil on a half-sheet pan. Place in the oven and cook for 30 minutes until the Brussels sprouts are slightly charred.
- Remove from the oven and toss Brussels sprouts in the balsamic vinegar.

ITALIAN SAUSAGES & PEPPERS

SERVINGS: 4-5

This sheet-pan dinner is fast, requires few ingredients, and tastes amazing.
Serve on a hoagie roll, tossed with pasta, or simply by themselves.

INGREDIENTS

- 1 red bell pepper, sliced
- 1 yellow bell pepper, sliced
- 1 green bell pepper, sliced
- 1 large onion, sliced
- 2 garlic cloves, minced
- 1/2 teaspoon salt
- 1/2 teaspoon black pepper
- 1/4 teaspoon red pepper flakes
- 1 tablespoon olive oil
- 1lb sweet or hot Italian sausage links
- Fresh basil, chopped

DIRECTIONS

- Preheat the oven to 425 degrees.
- Add the bell peppers, onion, garlic, salt, pepper, red pepper flakes to a half-sheet pan and toss with the olive oil, then lay the sausages on top. Bake in the oven for 25-30 minutes until the internal temperature reads 160 degrees. Top with basil.

CHOCOLATE-DIPPED SHORTBREAD COOKIES

MAKES: 14-16 Cookies

Crumbly and buttery cookies dipped in chocolate, what's not to love! These cookies are easy to make with ingredients you probably already have in your pantry. The perfect make-ahead dessert.

INGREDIENTS

- 1 cup unsalted butter, room temperature
- 1 teaspoon vanilla extract
- 1/2 cup confectioners' sugar
- 2 cups all-purpose flour
- 1/4 teaspoon salt
- 6oz semi-sweet chocolate
- Pecans, roughly chopped (optional)

DIRECTIONS

- In a stand mixer fitted with the paddle attachment, beat the butter and vanilla extract until smooth and creamy, about 3 minutes. Add in the confectioners' sugar and beat until incorporated, about 1 minute. With the mixer on low, slowly add in the flour and salt and mix until the dough comes together.

- Dump the dough onto a lightly floured surface and shape into a disc. Wrap the dough in plastic wrap and place in the refrigerator to chill for 30 minutes.

- Pre-heat the oven to 350 degrees and line a half-sheet pan with parchment paper.

- On a lightly floured surface, roll the dough out to 1/2-inch thick and cut with a 2-inch cookie cutter. Place the cookies on the half-sheet pan and then bake for 20-25 minutes until lightly browned. Let cool to room temperature.

- Melt the chocolate in a double boiler, then dip each cookie to coat half of it. Place back on the parchment paper and sprinkle with pecans.

CINNAMON ROLLS WITH CREAM CHEESE ICING

MAKES: 12 Cinnamon Rolls

These gooey, sticky cinnamon rolls are good for a delectable breakfast or scrumptious dessert.

INGREDIENTS

Cinnamon Rolls:

- 2/3 cup light brown sugar
- 1/4 cup sugar
- 1-1/2 tablespoons ground cinnamon
- 1/4 teaspoon salt
- 2 sheets puff pastry, thawed
- 3 tablespoons unsalted butter, melted

Cream Cheese Icing:

- 4oz cream cheese, room temperature
- 4 tablespoons unsalted butter, room temperature
- 1 cup confectioners' sugar
- 1 teaspoon vanilla extract
- 1/4 cup whole milk
- Chopped pecans or raisins for topping (optional)

DIRECTIONS

- Preheat the oven to 350 degrees. Line a half sheet pan with parchment paper.

- In a small bowl, add the brown sugar, sugar, cinnamon, and salt and stir to combine. Set aside.

- On a lightly floured surface, open up one sheet of puff pastry left to right. Brush the entire surface with butter. Sprinkle the puff pastry with half of the brown sugar mixture leaving a 1-inch space around the edge. Starting with the side closest to you, tightly roll the puff pastry away from you. Cut off the edges of the puff pastry. Cut the puff pastry in half, then cut each half into thirds yielding 6 rolls. Place the rolls on the baking sheet upright. Repeat for the second sheet.

- Bake at 350 degrees for 30-35 minutes until the rolls are lightly browned. Remove from the oven and let cool slightly.

- For the cream cheese icing, add the cream cheese and butter to a stand mixer fitted with the paddle attachment and beat until smooth. Gradually add the confectioners' sugar and vanilla extract and beat until combined. With the mixer on low, slowly add the milk until combined. Spread the icing over the cinnamon rolls. Top with pecans or raisins if using.

BEEF WELLINGTON

SERVINGS: 6-8

TOOLS OF THE TRADE

Digital Meat Thermometer: My newest and favorite tool! Gone are the days of having to manually check to see if the meat is done. A digital meat thermometer syncs directly to your smartphone and alerts you the moment the meat is done.

One of my favorite TV shows is "Hell's Kitchen". I like it not only for the drama of Gordon Ramsay screaming at people, but also for the amazing food the he and the chefs produce. The one dish they make on the show that's always made my mouth water is the Beef Wellington. After years of craving it, I finally got my chance to eat it at none other than the Hell's Kitchen restaurant in Las Vegas. It was everything I had dreamed and more! I knew I had to go home and make it for myself.

This elegant dish is not something the everyday person will make on a weekly basis because it's very expensive; however, it's the perfect meal to serve on holidays and special occasions.

INGREDIENTS

- 2-3lb beef tenderloin, trimmed
- Salt
- Black pepper
- 3 tablespoons olive oil
- 2 tablespoons Dijon mustard
- 8oz portabella mushrooms, sliced

- 1/4 cup shallots, diced
- 1 teaspoon fresh thyme, chopped
- 3 garlic cloves, minced
- 5-6 thin slices of prosciutto
- 1 sheet puff pastry, thawed
- 1 egg beaten
- Sea salt

DIRECTIONS

- Tie the beef in 3 places with kitchen twine so that it holds a cylinder shape. Season the beef with salt and black pepper on all sides.

- Add the olive oil to a frying pan or skillet over high heat. Once the oil is hot, sear the beef on all sides, then remove from the heat. Cut the twine and brush the beef with the Dijon mustard and set aside.

- Turn the heat to medium and add the mushrooms, shallots, and thyme to the pan and cook for 5 minutes until browned and tender. Add in the garlic and cook for 1 minute. Remove from the heat and set aside to cool slightly. Add the mushroom mixture to the bowl of a food processor and process until finely processed.

- Layer the prosciutto on a sheet of plastic wrap, then sprinkle the prosciutto with black pepper. Next, spread the mushroom mixture over top of the prosciutto. Place the beef tenderloin in the center of the mushroom mixture, then roll the prosciutto and mushrooms over the beef using the plastic wrap to form a log. Twist the ends tight to form a cylinder shape and place in the refrigerator for 30 minutes to firm up.

- Preheat the oven to 425 degrees. Line a half-sheet pan with parchment paper.

- On a lightly floured surface, roll out the puff pastry to encompass the beef, about 12x12in. Remove the plastic wrap from the beef, then place in the center of the puff pastry and brush the edges of the pastry with the beaten egg. Fold the pastry around the beef cutting off any excess pastry. Tightly wrap the pastry-wrapped beef in plastic wrap twisting the ends and place in the refrigerator for 10 minutes.

- Remove the plastic wrap and brush the pastry with the beaten egg and score the pastry with the back of a paring knife. Sprinkle the top of the pastry with sea salt and place on the half-sheet pan. Place the sheet pan in the oven and cook until the internal temperature reads 125 degrees on an instant read thermometer, about 45 minutes. Remove the beef from the oven and let rest for 15 minutes before carving.

ELECTRIC PRESSURE COOKER

One of the newest and most popular kitchen appliances to hit the mainstream in the last ten years is the electric pressure cooker. It seems like everyone has gone crazy over these things! There are a plethora of cookbooks, blogs, and websites dedicated to this culinary newbie.

These energy-efficient machines use high pressure and heat to cook, which helps fast flavor development and reduces cooking time by 70% from other cooking methods.

They're not just used for pressure cooking. Many cookers on the market have several functions such as sauté, rice cooker, and slow cooker. When I first bought my electric pressure cooker, I didn't use it very often because honestly, I was a little intimidated by the thing and afraid it would literally blow up in my face. They may seem scary, but they're completely safe. These cookers have sensors that help regulate the internal pressure and temperature and will ensure that the lid is securely closed. If the lid is not on properly, then the machine will not come to pressure. These little guys are definitely not your grandma's stovetop pressure cookers.

Once I got comfortable with my cooker, I found myself using it all the time. The hands-off cooking makes preparing meals so much easier! Also, they make for very easy clean up (major plus for me)!

For the purpose of these recipes, I used a 6-quart Instant Pot electric pressure cooker. Six quarts is the most popular size, but you can go smaller and bigger. Get the size that best fits your needs.

If you're new to cooking with an electric pressure cooker, there are two things that I always tell people to remember to do to ensure cooking is successful. (1) Make sure the rubber sealing ring around the lid is secure and intact. If not, the cooker won't come to pressure. (2) Make sure that the steam valve is closed. If the valve is open, steam will release and the cooker won't come too pressure.

There are literally thousands of recipes for electric pressure cookers. The ones that I included here are the ones that I use all the time. I'm always scouring the internet for new things to make in the bad boy.

BEEF STEW

SERVINGS: 4-6

A traditional comfort food that's packed with tender meat and vegetables that are enveloped in a rich wine sauce. Cold weather essential eating at its finest!

INGREDIENTS

- 1-1/2 - 2lbs beef chuck roast, cubed
- Salt
- Black pepper
- 2 tablespoons vegetable oil
- 2 garlic cloves, minced
- 1/3 cup red wine
- 1lb russet potatoes, peeled and cut into 1-in cubes

- 2 carrots, chopped
- 1 medium onion, diced
- 6 cups beef stock
- 1 tablespoon Worcestershire sauce
- 2-3 sprigs of fresh thyme and rosemary tied together with kitchen twine
- 1/2 teaspoon red pepper flakes
- 1 tablespoon cornstarch

DIRECTIONS

- Season the beef with salt and pepper to taste. Set the cooker to the sauté function on high heat and add the vegetable oil. Once the oil is hot, add the beef and sear for 2-3 minutes each side. Add the garlic and cook for 1 minute. Stir in the red wine and cook for 2-3 minutes. Add the potatoes, carrots, onion, beef stock, Worcestershire sauce, rosemary and thyme, red pepper flakes, and salt and pepper to taste.

- Place the lid on the cooker and set to pressure cook for 30 minutes. Once the time is up, let the steam release naturally for 10 minutes, then manually release the rest of the pressure. Remove the lid and discard the rosemary and thyme.

- Set the cooker back to the sauté function on medium heat. In a small bowl, whisk together the cornstarch with 1 tablespoon water and add to the pot. Simmer for several minutes until the stew is thickened.

CORN ON THE COB

SERVINGS: 4-8

Corn on the cob is one of my all-time favorite sides! Fresh delicious corn in minutes!

INGREDIENTS

- 1 cup water
- 4-8 ears of corn,
  husks and silks removed
- Unsalted butter
- Table salt

DIRECTIONS

Place the water in the pressure cooker, then place a trivet in the bottom. Place the ears of corn on the trivet and close the lid. Pressure cook for 2 minutes, then quick release the pressure. Serve hot topped with butter and salt.

WHITE RICE

MAKES: Approximately 3 Cups

Foolproof rice in half the time it takes on the stovetop.

INGREDIENTS

- 1 cup white rice
- 1 cup chicken stock or water
- 1 tablespoon unsalted butter
- 1/2 teaspoon salt
- Several sprigs of fresh thyme (optional)

DIRECTIONS

Add all ingredients to the pressure cooker and set to pressure cook for 4 minutes. Once finished, allow the steam to release naturally for 10 minutes, then quick release the rest. Discard the thyme sprigs.

BROWN RICE

MAKES: Approximately 3 Cups

Perfect, fluffy brown rice made in no time.

INGREDIENTS

- 1 cup brown rice
- 1-1/2 cups chicken stock or water
- Pinch of salt
- 1 tablespoon unsalted butter

DIRECTIONS

Add the brown rice, stock/water, salt, and butter to the pressure cooker and close the lid. Set to pressure cook for 20 minutes. When the time is up, let the pressure release naturally. Remove the lid and fluff the rice with a fork.

"TAKE-OUT" GENERAL TSO'S CHICKEN

TOOLS OF THE TRADE

Garlic Press: Easily mince garlic in no time without the sticky fingers.

SERVINGS: 4

A fast and healthy take on the classic Chinese take-out favorite.

INGREDIENTS

- 1/2 cup soy sauce
- 1/4 cup hoisin sauce
- 2 tablespoons rice vinegar
- 1 tablespoon peanut butter
- 1 tablespoon honey
- 2 tablespoons brown sugar
- 2 garlic cloves, minced
- 1 teaspoon fresh ginger, grated
- 1/2 teaspoon red pepper flakes
- 2lbs chicken breast or thighs, cut into bite sized pieces
- 4 tablespoons corn starch, divided
- 2 tablespoons sesame oil
- Sesame seeds
- Green onions, chopped

DIRECTIONS

- In a medium-sized bowl, whisk together the soy sauce, hoisin sauce, rice vinegar, peanut butter, honey, brown sugar, garlic, ginger, and red pepper flakes and set aside.

- In another medium bowl, toss together the chicken and 3 tablespoons of cornstarch.

- Set the cooker to the sauté setting over medium heat and add in the sesame oil. Once the oil is hot, add the chicken and cook until lightly browned, about 5 minutes.

- Stir in the sauce, then close the lid. Set to pressure cook for 5 minutes. Allow the steam to release naturally for 10 minutes, then manually release the rest of the steam.

- Turn the cooker to the sauté function over medium heat. In a small bowl, whisk together 1 tablespoon corn starch and 1/4 cup hot water. Add to the pot and cook for 1-2 minutes until the sauce is thickened. Serve hot with rice and steamed broccoli topped with sesame seeds and green onions.

CHICKEN STOCK

MAKES: 2 Quarts

I've often heard that nothing beats homemade chicken stock. I've always just bought it in the store up until I actually made it for myself. Wow, what a difference! I often make this from the carcass of a chicken I cooked for supper and leftover vegetables.

INGREDIENTS

- 2-1/2 - 3lbs chicken wings and backbones or carcass of a roasted chicken
- 1 medium onion, quartered
- 2 whole carrots, roughly chopped
- 2 celery stalks, roughly chopped
- 1 head garlic, cut in half crosswise
- 5-6 sprigs fresh dill
- 5-6 sprigs fresh parsley
- 5-6 sprigs fresh thyme
- 2 bay leaves
- 2 teaspoons salt
- 1 teaspoon whole peppercorns
- 7 cups water

DIRECTIONS

- Place all ingredients into the pressure cooker. Close and lock the lid and set to pressure cook for 40 minutes. When the time is up, release the pressure and remove the lid. Strain the stock over a colander and discard the solids.

- Store in an air tight container for 3 days in the refrigerator or 3 months in the freezer.

MASHED POTATOES WITH GARLIC HERB BUTTER

SERVINGS: 6

These no-fuss mashed potatoes are bursting in flavor with the savory garlic and herb butter. Not your mama's mashed potatoes!

INGREDIENTS

- 3lbs russet potatoes, peeled and cut into 1-inch cubes
- 5 cups chicken stock or water
- 3/4 cup whole milk
- 6 tablespoons unsalted butter
- 3 garlic cloves, smashed
- Several sprigs fresh rosemary and thyme
- Salt
- Black Pepper
- Chives, chopped

DIRECTIONS

- Add the potatoes and chicken stock/water to the pressure cooker. Place the lid on the cooker and set to pressure cook for 8 minutes.

- While the potatoes are cooking, add the milk, butter, garlic, and herbs to a small saucepan over low heat. Heat until the butter is melted and the mixture is hot. Discard the garlic and herbs with a slotted spoon.

- When the time on the cooker is up, manually release the pressure and remove the lid. Strain the potatoes and return back to the pot. Add the butter mixture and salt and pepper to taste to the potatoes and mash to desired consistency. Serve hot, topped with chives.

SOUTHERN BLACK-EYED PEAS

SERVINGS: 6-8

This classic dish is cooked with ham and bacon to maximize flavor. The best part about these peas is that they are ready in no time, thanks to an electric pressure cooker. Gone are the days of having to soak dried beans overnight! The perfect side to serve on New Year's Day to bring good luck all year!

INGREDIENTS

- olive oil
- 4 garlic cloves, minced
- 6 cups chicken stock
- 1lb dry black-eyed peas, rinsed
- 1/2lb ham hock
- 3 strips bacon
- 1 teaspoon black pepper
- 2 bay leaves

DIRECTIONS

- Set the cooker to the sauté function over medium heat and add about 1 teaspoon of olive oil. Add the garlic and cook for 1 minute. Add the chicken stock and scrape any browned bits in the bottom of the pot. Add the black-eyed peas, ham hock, bacon strips, pepper, and bay leaves and place the lid on the cooker. Set to pressure cook for 25 minutes.

- When the cooking cycle ends, let the pressure release naturally for 15 minutes, then release the rest of the pressure manually. Discard the ham hock and bay leaves.

MUSHROOM RISOTTO

SERVINGS: 4-6

I love risotto, but it requires so much attention to cook. Traditional risotto is made by ladling liquid stock in the risotto every few minutes while having to stir constantly so the risotto doesn't stick. Who has time for that? With an electric pressure cooker, you just get together the ingredients, close the lid, and walk away! In no time, you'll have a warm bowl of creamy rich risotto people will think you spent hours slaving over!

INGREDIENTS

- 6 tablespoons unsalted butter
- 1/2 cup shallots, diced
- 2 cups mushrooms, roughly chopped
- 1 teaspoon fresh thyme, chopped
- 2 garlic cloves, minced
- 1/2 cup white wine
- 2 cups Arborio rice
- 4 cups chicken stock
- 1/2 cup frozen sweet peas
- 1-1/2 teaspoons salt
- 1/2 teaspoon black pepper
- 1 cup freshly shredded Parmesan cheese, plus extra for topping
- Fresh parsley, roughly chopped

DIRECTIONS

- Set the pressure cooker to the sauté function on medium heat and add the butter. Once the butter is melted, add the shallots, mushrooms, and thyme and cook for 5 minutes until tender. Add the garlic and cook for 1 minute. Add the wine and cook for 3-4 minutes until the wine is slightly reduced. Add in the rice and stir to coat, then add the chicken stock, sweet peas, salt, and pepper.

- Place the lid on the cooker and set to pressure cook on high for 5 minutes. Once the time is up, release the pressure. Stir in the Parmesan cheese until melted. Serve hot topped with extra Parmesan cheese and parsley.

ROASTED PEPPER CHILI

SERVINGS: 6-8

A great pot of chili full of vibrant spices and textures that can be made in under an hour. The roasted poblano peppers gives this chili a touch of sweetness that blends perfectly with the other ingredients.

INGREDIENTS

- 2 poblano peppers
- Olive oil
- 1 medium onion, diced
- 4 garlic cloves, minced
- 12oz can of beer, such as lager
- 2lbs ground beef, browned and drained
- 1 yellow bell pepper, diced
- 1 jalapeño pepper, diced (seeded for less heat)
- 2 tablespoons chili powder
- 1 teaspoon coriander
- 1 teaspoon ground cumin
- 1 teaspoon onion powder

- 1 teaspoon paprika
- 1 teaspoon salt
- 1/2 teaspoon black pepper
- 1/2 teaspoon cayenne pepper
- 8oz can tomato sauce
- 6oz can tomato paste
- 15oz can diced tomatoes
- 15oz can kidney beans, drained
- 3/4 cup beef stock
- Green onions
- Sour cream
- Shredded cheese

DIRECTIONS

- Preheat the oven to 500 degrees. Brush the poblano peppers with olive oil, then place the peppers in the oven and roast for 8-10 minutes on each side until slightly charred. Remove from the oven and when the peppers are cool enough to handle, peel the skin off, roughly chop, and set aside.

- Set the cooker to the sauté setting over medium heat and add 1 tablespoon of olive oil to the pot. When the oil is hot, add the onions and cook until soft and translucent, about 5 minutes. Add the garlic and cook for 1 minute. Add the beer and cook for 10 minutes until the beer reduces by half.

- Add the ground beef, poblano peppers, yellow bell pepper, jalapeño pepper, spices, tomato sauce, tomato paste, diced tomatoes, kidney beans, and the beef stock. Place the lid on and set to cook for 20 minutes. When finished, let the pressure release naturally for 15 minutes, then manually release the remaining pressure. Serve hot topped with green onions, sour cream, and shredded cheese.

NEW ENGLAND CLAM CHOWDER

SERVINGS: 4

A perfect bowl of comfort! This satisfying soup is full of tender clams and creamy potatoes. Ideal for a cold winter day and it's budget friendly.

INGREDIENTS

- 4 slices bacon, chopped
- 4 tablespoons unsalted butter
- 1 medium onion, diced
- 1 teaspoon fresh thyme, chopped
- 3 garlic cloves, minced
- 4 cups seafood stock
- 2 carrots, diced
- 2 celery stalks, diced
- 2 russet potatoes, diced
- 1 bay leaf
- 1 teaspoon salt
- 1/2 teaspoon black pepper
- (3) 6.5oz cans clams with juice
- 2 cups half-&-half
- Fresh parsley, chopped

DIRECTIONS

- Set the cooker to the sauté setting over medium heat. Once hot, add the bacon and cook until browned, about 5 minutes. Remove the bacon with a slotted spoon and set aside.

- Add the butter, onions, and thyme and cook until soft and translucent, about 5 minutes. Add the garlic and cook for 1 minute. Add the seafood stock and deglaze the pot by scraping the browned bits from the bottom. Add the carrots, celery, potatoes, bay leaf, salt, pepper, and clams. Place the lid on the pressure cooker and set to pressure cook for 8 minutes. Once the time is up, manually release the pressure. Remove the lid and discard the bay leaf.

- Set the cooker back to the sauté setting over medium heat a add the half-&-half to the pot and simmer for 5 minutes. Serve hot topped with bacon and parsley.

STEAMED CRAB LEGS

SERVES: 2-4

I always thought crab legs sounded so intimidating and complicated to make that I just never even bothered trying, but nothing could be further from the truth. It's legit the easiest thing in the world to make, especially with an electric pressure cooker. In minutes, you'll be enjoying this classic buttery shellfish. You can even cook them straight from frozen.

INGREDIENTS

- 1 cup water
- Juice from 1 lemon
- 4 garlic cloves, smashed
- 2-3lbs crab legs, fresh or frozen
- 1/2 cup unsalted butter, melted
- 1 teaspoon Old Bay seasoning

DIRECTIONS

- Add the water, lemon juice, and garlic to the pressure cooker. Place a trivet in the quick cooker and then place the crab legs on top of the trivet. Close the lid and pressure cook for 2 minutes for fresh crab legs or 4 minutes for frozen. When done, quick release the pressure. Serve crab legs hot.

- In a small bowl, whisk together the melted butter and Old Bay seasoning for dipping.

PASTA FORMULA

MAKES: 1 Pound

Perfectly al dente pasta in half the time it takes on the stovetop.

INGREDIENTS

- 1lb box pasta
- Salt to taste

DIRECTIONS

- Add the pasta, salt, and enough water to cover the pasta to the pressure cooker and close the lid.
- Determine the cook time using the formula below.
- Manually release the pressure once finished.

$$(\text{Box Time} \div 2) - 1 = \text{Cook Time}$$
Round any halves to the nearest even number (i.e. 3.5 rounds to 4)

FRUITS & VEGGIES	COOK TIME
Apples	1-2 minutes
Asparagus	1-2 minutes
Broccoli	0-1 minute (3 minutes for frozen)
Brussels Sprouts	2-3 minutes (4 minutes for frozen)
Cabbage	6 minutes
Carrots	3-4 minutes (6-8 for frozen)
Cauliflower Florets	2-3 minutes
Green Beans	2-3 minutes
Mixed Vegetables	3-4 minutes
Sweet Potatoes (cubed)	2-3 minutes

MEATS	COOK TIME
Beef Roast	35-40 minutes
Chicken Breast	8-10 minutes
Chicken Thighs	10-12 minutes
Chicken Whole	20-25 minutes
Chicken Wings	8-10 minutes
Fish Fillet	2-3 minutes
Pork Chops	12-15 minutes
Pork Ribs	20-25 minutes
Shrimp	1-2 minutes

MISCELLANEOUS	COOK TIME
Hard Boiled Eggs	4 minutes
Quick Oats	1 minute

AIR FRYER

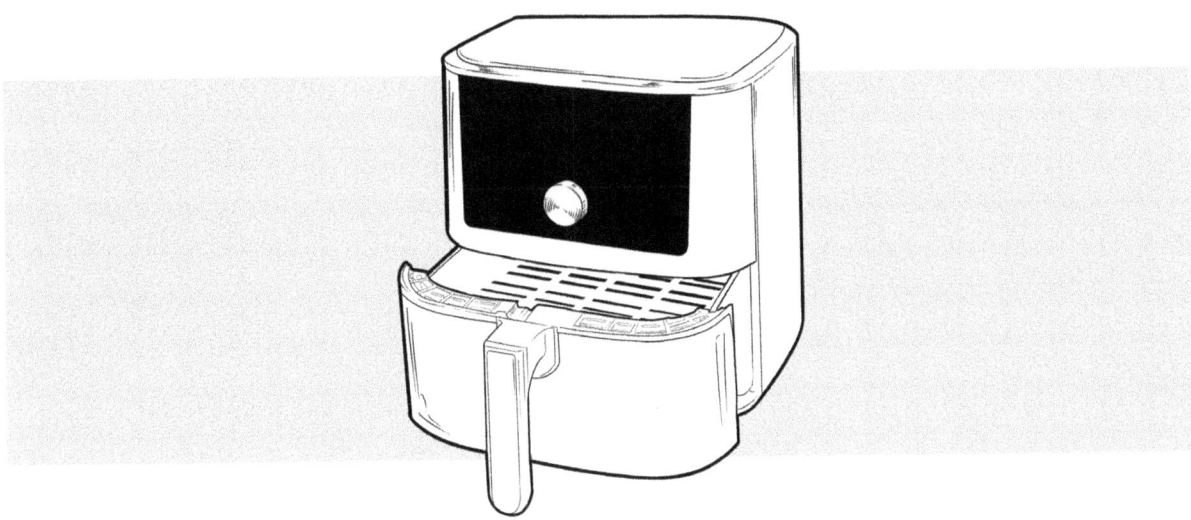

One of the most popular trends in kitchen appliances out now is an air fryer. There are countless brands and versions out there to choose from and they are a must-have for busy people who are constantly on the go because they cook food good and fast.

An air fryer is a mini countertop convection oven that constantly circulates intense heat that makes for quick cooking. You can cook something in an air fryer in the same amount of time that it takes to preheat a traditional oven.

The price of an air fryer can range from under $100 to several hundreds of dollars, depending on the size and features you want. The more expensive air fryers can also double as a rotisserie and dehydrator. They also have a wide variety of accessories and attachments such as baking pans, baskets for fries and skewers for kabobs. There's a never-ending list of the things you can make in this baby!

The best, and most popular pro of an air fryer is healthier cooking. Air fryers use a lot less oil than deep frying and you still get that great taste and crispiness. For most recipes, the most oil you need is about a tablespoon. They can cut the calories by 70-80%.

Another reason people love air fryers so much is how fast they cook. The air fryer circulates the hot air in the small oven which reduces cooking time compared to a regular oven.

While air fryers are perfect for cooking things like fries and chicken nuggets, they are also great for baking desserts and easily reheating things like cold pizza. While the things that you can do with an air fryer you can do with a traditional home range and they do take up counter space, these are great to have because they are fast, efficient, and will cut cooking times in half. I find myself reaching for my air fryer more often that reaching to pre-heat the oven.

CHICKEN NUGGETS

MAKES: 20-24 Nuggets

Healthy kid-friendly supper that's easy and effortless.

INGREDIENTS

- 2 boneless skinless chicken breasts
- 1 cup all-purpose flour
- 1 teaspoon salt
- 1/2 teaspoon black pepper
- 1 teaspoon garlic powder
- 1/2 teaspoon paprika
- 2 eggs
- Hot sauce
- 2 cups Italian bread crumbs
- 2 tablespoons grated Parmesan cheese
- Cooking oil spray

DIRECTIONS

- Preheat the air fryer to 375 degrees for 10 minutes.
- Place the chicken breasts in a plastic bag and pound out with a meat tenderizer so that each breast is the same thickness. Remove from the plastic bag and cut the chicken into 2-inch pieces.
- Add the flour, salt, black pepper, garlic powder, and paprika to a medium-size bowl and stir to mix together. In a second medium sized bowl, whisk together the eggs, several dashes of hot sauce, and 2 tablespoons of water. In a third medium-sized bowl, add the bread crumbs, Parmesan cheese, and a pinch of salt.
- Dredge the chicken pieces in the flour, then the egg mixture, and finally the bread crumbs. Spray each side of the chicken pieces with cooking oil.
- Spray the basket of the air fryer with cooking oil. Working in batches, place the chicken in the basket and cook on 375 for 8-10 minutes, flipping halfway through.

BUFFALO CAULIFLOWER BITES

SERVINGS: 4-6

This healthy snack/appetizer is packed with great flavor and texture.

INGREDIENTS

- 1 head cauliflower, cut into florets
- 1 teaspoon garlic powder
- 1/2 teaspoon salt
- 1/4 teaspoon black pepper
- 2 tablespoons olive oil
- 1/2 cup Buffalo sauce

DIRECTIONS

- In a large bowl, toss together the cauliflower, garlic powder, salt, pepper, and olive oil. Working in batches if needed, place the cauliflower in the air fryer basket and cook at 390 degrees for 15 minutes until tender.

- Toss the cauliflower in the Buffalo sauce. Serve with ranch or blue cheese dressing.

PORK TENDERLOIN

SERVINGS: 4

This is one of my favorite things to cook in the air fryer.
The flavors of the seasonings with the juicy lean meat are out of this world.

INGREDIENTS

- 4-5lb pork tenderloin
- 2-3 tablespoons olive oil
- 1 tablespoon salt
- 1/2 tablespoon black pepper
- 1 tablespoon garlic powder
- 2 tablespoons brown sugar
- 2 tablespoons fresh rosemary, chopped

DIRECTIONS

- Preheat the air fryer at 400 degrees for 5 minutes. Brush the pork loin with olive oil on all sides

- In a small bowl, mix together the salt, pepper, garlic powder, brown sugar, and rosemary. Apply the rub to the pork loin on all sides.

- Place the pork loin in the air fryer and cook for 35-40 minutes until the internal temperature reads 145 degrees, flipping halfway through.

- Remove the pork loin from the air fryer, wrap in aluminum foil, and let rest for 10 minutes before slicing.

TOOLS OF THE TRADE

Mortar & Pestle: Make amazing flavorful pastes and rubs.

BAKED POTATO

SERVINGS: 2

The air fryer makes "baking" potatoes so much faster and easier. In no time, you'll be enjoying a delicious baked potato that's tender on the inside and slightly crisp on the outside.

INGREDIENTS

- 2 baking potatoes
- Olive oil
- Salt
- Black pepper

DIRECTIONS

Punch several holes in the potatoes with a knife or fork. Brush the potatoes with olive oil and sprinkle with salt and pepper. Add to the air fryer and cook at 400 degrees for 40–50 minutes until fork-tender, flipping the potatoes halfway through. Serve hot.

BAKED SWEET POTATO

SERVINGS: 2

Delicious baked sweet potato that can be made sweet or savory...
the perfect side dish for a hearty autumn supper.

INGREDIENTS

- 2 sweet potatoes
- Olive oil
- Salt

DIRECTIONS

Punch several holes in the potatoes with a knife or fork. Brush the potatoes with olive oil and sprinkle with salt. Add to the air fryer and cook at 390 degrees for 45-50 minutes until fork-tender, flipping the potatoes halfway through. Serve hot.

FRENCH FRIES

SERVINGS: 2

The salty, flavorful, quintessential side dish that's healthier than deep frying.

INGREDIENTS

- 1-1-1/2 lbs russet potatoes, cut into fries
- 1/2 teaspoon salt
- 1/2 teaspoon black pepper
- 1 tablespoon vegetable oil

DIRECTIONS

Toss together the potatoes, salt, pepper, and vegetable oil, then add to the air fryer basket. Cook for 10 minutes at 350 degrees. When done, toss the fries, then cook for 20 minutes at 400 degrees tossing halfway through.

CHEESEBURGERS

SERVINGS: 4

Let's face it, burgers should only be cooked on a grill; however, it's not always possible to fire up the grill. The air fryer is the next best thing. In minutes, you'll have juicy, cheesy burgers cooked to perfection.

INGREDIENTS

- 1lb ground beef
- 1 teaspoon salt
- 1/2 teaspoon black pepper
- 1 teaspoon garlic powder
- 1/2 teaspoon onion powder
- 1/4 teaspoon cayenne pepper
- 1 tablespoon Worcestershire sauce
- 4 slices of cheese

DIRECTIONS

- Preheat the air fryer at 400 degrees for 5 minutes.

- In a medium bowl, combine all the ingredients except for the cheese and lightly mix with a fork. Shape the burgers into 4 patties.

- Cook the burgers at 400 degrees for 10 minutes flipping halfway through. Place a slice of cheese on top of each burger, then cook for 1 minute at 400 degrees until the cheese is melted.

CHEDDAR BISCUITS

MAKES: 6-7 Biscuits

Cheesy, buttery biscuits that are loaded with flavor. Perfect to cook in the air fryer if your oven is being used for something else. Everything is hot and ready at the same time!

INGREDIENTS

- 2 cups all-purpose flour
- 2 teaspoons baking powder
- 1 teaspoon sugar
- 1 teaspoon salt
- 1/2 teaspoon garlic powder

- 6 tablespoons cold unsalted butter, grated
- 1 cup cheddar cheese, shredded
- 3/4 cup buttermilk
- 2 tablespoons unsalted butter, melted

DIRECTIONS

- Preheat the air fryer at 390 degrees for 5 minutes and grease the cooking tray.

- In a large bowl, whisk together the flour, baking powder, sugar, salt, and garlic powder. Fold in the butter and cheese until combined. Stir in the buttermilk until the dough comes together.

- Dump out the dough onto a lightly floured surface and fold the dough over several times, then flatten out with your hands to a thickness of 1-inch. Cut out the biscuits using a 3-inch biscuit cutter.

- Place the biscuits on the tray and air fry at 390 degrees for 9-11 minutes until the biscuits are golden brown. Brush the biscuits with the melted butter.

CHICKEN QUESADILLA

MAKES: 1 Quesadilla

*These cheesy quesadillas are so fast to make and they taste amazing.
I often make these for lunch with chicken left over from the night before.*

INGREDIENTS

- 1/2 cup chicken breast, shredded, seasoned & cooked
- 1/2 cup shredded cheese
- 2 flour tortillas

DIRECTIONS

- Preheat the air fryer at 370 degrees for 3 minutes.

- Spray the pan with cooking spray then place one of the tortillas on the pan. Add the chicken and cheese then top with the other tortilla. Spray the top of the tortilla with cooking spray and place 4 toothpicks in the sides of the quesadilla so the top will not blow off during cooking.

- Cook at 370 degrees for 4 minutes, then flip the quesadilla and cook for an additional 4 minutes. Remove the toothpicks and serve warm.

FRIED ONION RINGS

SERVINGS: 2-3

Crispy and delicious...perfect for a quick snack or appetizer.

INGREDIENTS

- 1/2 cup all-purpose flour
- 1 teaspoon salt
- 1/2 teaspoon black pepper
- 1/2 cup buttermilk
- 1 egg
- Hot sauce
- 1-1/2 cups panko bread crumbs
- 1 large onion,
  cut into 1/2-inch slices

DIRECTIONS

- Pre-heat the air fryer at 400 degrees for 5 minutes.

- Whisk together the flour, salt, and pepper in a shallow bowl. In a second bowl, whisk together the buttermilk, egg, and several dashes of hot sauce. Add the bread crumbs to a third bowl.

- Dredge the onion slices in the flour shaking off any excess. Next, dredge the onions in the buttermilk mixture then in the panko crumbs.

- Spray the cooking basket with cooking oil. Working in batches, add the onion rings to the basket in a single layer. Cook on 400 degrees for 8-10 minutes until the onion rings are golden brown.

CHOCOLATE LAVA CAKES

SERVINGS: 4

Chocolaty, rich dessert that's cakey on the outside and gooey on the inside.
The perfect end to any meal! Goes great with a big scoop of vanilla ice cream!

INGREDIENTS

- 3 tablespoons flour
- 1/2 cup confectioners' sugar
- 1/8 teaspoon salt
- 2 eggs
- 2 egg yolks
- 1/2 cup unsalted butter
- 6oz semisweet chocolate
- 1 teaspoon vanilla extract

DIRECTIONS

- Grease 4 6oz ramekins and set aside.

- Sift together the flour, confectioners' sugar, and salt into a small bowl and set aside. Whisk the eggs and egg yolks together and set aside.

- In a double boiler, melt the butter and chocolate together. Stir in the vanilla. Next, fold in the flour mixture until combined, then mix in the eggs until incorporated. Evenly divide the batter between the ramekins.

- Place the ramekins in the basket of the air fryer and cook at 370 degrees for 8 minutes. When done, let sit for 1 minute, then serve immediately.

COCONUT SHRIMP

SERVINGS: 4

Golden, sweet, crispy coconut shrimp is always a crowd-pleasing favorite.

INGREDIENTS

- 1/2 cup corn starch
- 1 cup shredded coconut
- 1 cup panko bread crumbs
- 2 teaspoons paprika
- 2 teaspoons garlic powder
- 1 teaspoon salt
- 1 teaspoon black pepper
- 2 eggs
- 1lb large shrimp, peeled and deveined with tails removed
- Cooking oil spray

DIRECTIONS

- Preheat the air fryer at 390 degrees for 5 minutes.

- Add the cornstarch to a small bowl. In a second bowl, whisk the eggs and 1 tablespoon of water. In a third bowl, stir together the coconut, bread crumbs, paprika, garlic powder, salt, and black pepper until combined.

- Toss the shrimp in the corn starch shaking off any excess. Next, dip the shrimp in the eggs, then toss in the bread crumb mixture, pressing to coat thoroughly.

- Spray the air fryer pan with cooking spray. Working in batches, place the shrimp on the air fryer pan and spray each shrimp with the cooking spray. Cook at 390 degrees for 5 minutes, then flip the shrimp, spray each with cooking spray again, and cook for another 5 minutes.

JALAPEÑO CHEDDAR POPPERS

MAKES: 12 Poppers

These cheesy, spicy poppers are the easiest snack to make and they're ready in minutes. Perfect midnight snack!

INGREDIENTS

- 2/3 cup cheddar cheese, finely shredded
- 1/4 teaspoon salt
- 1/4 teaspoon black pepper
- 1/2 teaspoon garlic powder
- 6 jalapeño peppers, halved and seeded
- 3 tablespoons panko bread crumbs
- Bacon pieces
- Cooking oil spray

DIRECTIONS

- Preheat the air fryer at 380 degrees for 5 minutes.
- In a small bowl, combine the cheese, salt, black pepper, and garlic powder.
- Stuff each jalapeño pepper half with the cheese mixture, then top with bread crumbs and bacon pieces. Add jalapeño seeds for more heat. Spray each pepper with cooking spray.
- Spray the air fryer basket with cooking spray. Cooking in batches, place the peppers in the basket and cook at 380 degrees for 7 minutes until the cheese is melted and the bread crumbs are browned.

SWEET TEA MARINATED CHICKEN BREASTS

SERVINGS: 2

This chicken is tender and juicy thanks to the South's most famous beverage.

INGREDIENTS

- 2 boneless skinless chicken breasts
- 2 cups cold sweet tea
- 1-1/2 tablespoons fresh rosemary, chopped
- 1 teaspoon salt
- 1/2 teaspoon black pepper
- 3 garlic cloves, roughly chopped

DIRECTIONS

- Add the chicken breasts, sweet tea, rosemary, salt, pepper, and garlic to a large bowl or zipper-lock bag and set in the refrigerator for 8 hours to marinate.
- Preheat the air fryer at 380 degrees for 5 minutes. Place the chicken breasts in the basket of the air fryer and cook at 380 degrees for 18-20 minutes until the internal temperature reads 165 degrees, flipping once during cooking.

VEGETABLES	TEMP	COOK TIME
Asparagus	400°	5 minutes
Broccoli	400°	6 minutes
Brussels Sprouts	380°	15 minutes
Carrots	380°	15 minutes
Cauliflower	400°	12 minutes
Kale Leaves	375°	3-5 minutes
Squash	400°	12 minutes

MEATS	TEMP	COOK TIME
Bacon	400°	6-8 minutes
Chicken Nuggets (frozen)	400°	10 minutes
Hot Dogs	400°	6 minutes
Pork Chops	400°	12 minutes
Sausage (links)	390°	10 minutes
Sausage (patties)	390°	8-10 minutes

MISCELLANEOUS	TEMP	COOK TIME
French Fries (frozen)	400°	15-18 minutes
Mozzarella Sticks (frozen)	400°	8 minutes
Tater Tots (frozen)	400°	16-18 minutes

SLOW COOKER

Growing up, it seemed like everyone's family had a slow cooker. When I hear the term "slow cooker", I typically think of a bland roast and potatoes for Sunday lunch after church.

There's so much more to the humble slow cooker than boring, bland meals. They can produce the most amazing and succulent dishes that range from wholesome family dinners to fancy gourmet cuisine.

Because slow cookers obviously slow cook food, they are great for tenderizing meat, making them smooth and extra tender. The slow cooking process also allows for more distribution of flavors making dishes really pop.

With just a handful of ingredients, you can make so many amazing things in a slow cooker such as dips, soups, stews, casseroles, and one-pot meals.

The best thing about a slow cooker is the convenience. Whole meals can be made completely unattended. When you know you have a busy, exhausting day ahead, simply gather all the ingredients in the slow cooker, let cook all day, and you can come home to a warm, comforting meal ready as soon as you walk in the door.

Another great thing about slow cookers is how easy they are to clean. If you're like me and even hate having to scrub just one pot, slow cooker liners are life changing! Cleaning the kitchen can't get any easier.

Slow cookers come in a wide variety of versions and sizes. They are relatively inexpensive, too.

If you're a busy person who likes to make great meals with little to no effort, a slow cooker is the perfect piece of equipment.

SLOPPY JOES

SERVINGS: 8

Everyone's childhood favorite! An amazingly simple, delicious meal with a sauce that's leaps and bounds better than the canned stuff. A family favorite for all ages.

INGREDIENTS

- 2lbs ground beef
- 1 tablespoon olive oil
- 1 small onion, diced
- 1 bell pepper, diced
- 1 teaspoon fresh thyme, chopped
- 3 garlic cloves, minced
- 28oz can tomato sauce
- 1/2 cup ketchup
- 2 tablespoons Worcestershire sauce
- 2 tablespoons brown sugar
- 1 teaspoon salt
- 1 teaspoon black pepper
- 1 teaspoon dried oregano
- 1 teaspoon chili powder
- 1/4 teaspoon cumin
- Hamburger buns

DIRECTIONS

- In a large frying pan, brown the ground beef, then drain the grease. Wipe the pan clean, then add the olive oil over medium heat. Once the oil is hot, add the onions, bell pepper, and thyme and cook for 3-4 minutes until tender. Add the garlic and cook for 1 minute, then remove from the heat.

- Add the browned ground beef, onions and peppers, tomato sauce, ketchup, Worcestershire sauce, brown sugar, salt, pepper, oregano, chili powder, and cumin to the slow cooker. Cook on low for 6 hours or on high for 3 hours. Serve hot on hamburger buns.

EASTERN NC-STYLE PULLED PORK

SERVINGS: 12-16

The tangy, vinegar-based BBQ sauce is the perfect complement to the smoky-flavored meat.

INGREDIENTS

- 3 cups apple cider vinegar
- 1/4 cup brown sugar
- 1 tablespoon ketchup
- 1 teaspoon salt
- 1 teaspoon black pepper
- 1 tablespoon red pepper flakes
- 1/2 teaspoon cayenne pepper
- 1 medium onion, diced
- 4-6lb pork shoulder, trimmed of excess fat
- 1 tablespoon liquid smoke

DIRECTIONS

- In a medium-sized pot, add the apple cider vinegar, brown sugar, ketchup, salt, black pepper, red pepper flakes, and cayenne pepper and simmer on low heat for 15 minutes. Add the onions to the slow cooker, then the pork shoulder. Pour the liquid smoke over top of the pork then pour in half of the BBQ sauce. Cook on low for 8-10 hours or high for 5-6 hours, until the pork shreds easily.

- When done, remove the pork from the slow cooker and shred or chop into barbecue and toss with several ladles of cooking juices. Serve with reserved BBQ sauce.

ALL-DAY POT ROAST

SERVINGS: 6-8

Everyone loves pot roast! A conventional, soothing meal slow cooked all day to absolute perfection.

INGREDIENTS

- 2-1/2 - 3lb chuck roast
- Salt
- Black Pepper
- Olive oil
- 1/2 cup red wine
- 2 tablespoons Worcestershire sauce
- 1-1/2 cups beef stock
- 2lbs Yukon Gold potatoes, quartered
- 3 whole carrots, cut into chunks
- 2 celery stalks, diced
- 1 medium onion, sliced
- 5 garlic cloves, minced
- 1 teaspoon fresh ginger, grated
- 2 tablespoons corn starch

DIRECTIONS

- Pat the chuck roast dry with a paper towel and season liberally with salt and pepper on all sides. Add 2 tablespoons olive oil to a large frying pan or skillet over medium-high heat. Sear the roast for 3-4 minutes on each side, then remove from the heat and set aside. Add the wine to the pan and scrape the bottom to delgaze, then stir in the Worcestershire sauce and beef stock. Remove from heat and set aside.

- Add the potatoes, carrots, celery, onion, garlic, and ginger to the slow cooker. Place the roast on top of the vegetables, then pour the beef stock mixture on top of the roast.

- Cook on low for 8-9 hours.

- To make the gravy, strain the juices from the bowl of the slow cooker into a medium-sized sauce pan over medium heat. Once hot, add about 1/2 cup of the liquid to a small bowl and whisk in the corn starch. Add back to the sauce pan and simmer for 5 minutes until the gravy thickens.

BROCCOLI AND CHEESE SOUP

SERVINGS: 5-6

This rich, creamy, and cheesy soup is a cinch to make and it's full with simple, flavorful ingredients. Slow cooked, yet cooks fast to make the perfect lunch on a cold day.

INGREDIENTS

- 4 cups fresh broccoli florets
- 1/2 cup onion, diced
- 1 cup carrots, chopped
- 2 garlic cloves, minced
- 1-1/2 teaspoons salt
- 1 teaspoon black pepper
- 1/4 teaspoon celery salt
- 5 cups chicken stock
- 3 tablespoons unsalted butter
- 1/4 cup all-purpose flour
- 1 cup half and half
- 2 cups cheddar cheese, shredded

DIRECTIONS

- Add the broccoli, onion, carrots, garlic, salt, pepper, celery salt, and chicken stock to the slow cooker and set to cook on low for 4 hours.

- When done, set the slow cooker to high.

- Add the butter to a saucepan over medium heat. When the butter is melted, whisk in the flour for one minute until the flour turns light brown. Slowly whisk in a ladle of the soup, then the half and half. Stir in the cheese until melted. Add the cheese mixture to the soup and stir to combine. Serve hot.

CHEESY SCALLOPED POTATOES

SERVINGS: 6-8

Slow cooked tender, cheesy potatoes are the perfect side for any meal.

INGREDIENTS

- 3lbs russet potatoes, peeled and sliced 1/4-inch thick
- 1/2 cup unsalted butter
- 3 garlic cloves, minced
- 1/2 cup all-purpose flour
- 1 cup whole milk
- Salt
- Black pepper
- 1/4 teaspoon ground nutmeg
- 1 cup Parmesan cheese, shredded
- 1/4 cup mascarpone cheese
- 1 cup Gruyere cheese
- Green onions, roughly chopped

DIRECTIONS

- Place the potatoes in the bowl of the slow cooker.
- In a medium-sized sauce pan, add the butter over medium heat. Once the butter is melted, add the garlic and cook for 1 minute. Whisk in the flour until it's absorbed, then slowly whisk in the milk. Add in 1 teaspoon salt, 1/2 teaspoon black pepper, nutmeg, Parmesan cheese, and mascarpone cheese and whisk until the cheese is melted in. Pour the cheese mixture over the potatoes. Add 1 teaspoon salt, 1/2 teaspoon black pepper, and the Gruyere cheese over the potatoes.
- Cook on high for 4-5 hours until the potatoes are tender. Top with green onions.

CHICKEN FAJITAS

SERVINGS: 6

An easy, no-hassle Mexican classic!

INGREDIENTS

- 2 teaspoons salt
- 1 teaspoon black pepper
- 2 teaspoons chili powder
- 1 teaspoon paprika
- 1 teaspoon onion powder
- 1/2 teaspoon cumin
- 1/4 teaspoon coriander
- 2lbs boneless, skinless chicken breast
- 14.5oz can diced tomatoes
- 1 onion, sliced
- 1 green bell pepper, sliced
- 1 yellow bell pepper, sliced
- 1 red bell pepper, sliced
- 4 garlic cloves, minced
- Zest and juice of 2 limes

DIRECTIONS

- In a small bowl, stir together the salt, black pepper, chili powder, paprika, onion powder, cumin, and coriander and set aside.
- Season both sides of the chicken with half of the spice mixture, then place in the slow cooker. Next, add the diced tomatoes, onion, bell peppers, garlic, and lime zest and juice and top with the rest of the spice mix.
- Cook on low for 4-6 hours or high for 2-3 hours until the vegetables are tender and the internal temperature of the chicken reads 165 degrees.
- Remove the chicken and cut into slices, then add back to the slow cooker. Serve hot on flour tortillas topped with cheese, sour cream, and cilantro.

HOMESTYLE CHICKEN NOODLE SOUP

SERVINGS: 8-10

Sick day or just a cold night...this soup is good for what ales ya!

INGREDIENTS

- 3 boneless, skinless chicken breasts
- Salt
- Black pepper
- 1 medium onion, diced
- 3 celery stalks, diced
- 3 whole carrots, diced
- 3 garlic cloves, minced
- 1 teaspoon fresh thyme, chopped
- 1 bay leaf
- 8 cups chicken stock
- 3 cups egg noodles
- Fresh parsley, chopped

DIRECTIONS

- Season the chicken breasts with salt and black pepper to taste and place them in the slow cooker. Add the onion, celery, carrots, garlic, thyme, bay leaf, 1 teaspoon salt, 1 teaspoon black pepper, and the chicken stock. Cook on low for 8 hours or high for 4 hours.

- Remove and discard the bay leaf. Remove the chicken breasts and shred the meat with 2 forks. Turn the slow cooker to high and add in the shredded chicken and egg noodles and cook for 10 minutes until the noodles are tender. Serve hot, garnished with parsley.

HONEY BUFFALO CHICKEN WINGS

TOOLS OF THE TRADE

Spice Grinder: Perfect for grinding spices, pepper, and coffee to enjoy fresh ground seasonings.

SERVINGS: 4-5

Cooking chicken wings in the slow cooker eliminates the mess from deep frying or grilling them. These wings are slow cooked in a sweet and spicy sauce until they're completely tender. The perfect snack for game day!

INGREDIENTS

- 2 tablespoons brown sugar
- 1 teaspoon chili powder
- 1-1/2 teaspoons salt
- 1 teaspoon black pepper
- 1-1/2 teaspoons onion powder
- 1 teaspoon paprika
- 1/2 teaspoon cumin

- 1/2 teaspoon ground ginger
- 4-5lbs chicken wings
- 1 cup hot sauce
- 1/2 cup honey
- 1 tablespoon molasses
- 2 tablespoons unsalted butter, melted
- 4 garlic cloves, minced
- 2 tablespoons corn starch

DIRECTIONS

- In a small bowl, stir together the brown sugar, chili powder, salt, pepper, onion powder, paprika, cumin, and ground ginger. Toss the chicken wings with the dry rub and place in the slow cooker.

- In a small bowl, whisk together the hot sauce, honey, molasses, butter, and garlic and pour over the chicken wings. Cook on low for 4 hours or high for 2 to 2-1/2 hours until the internal temperature of the chicken reads 165 degrees.

- Set the oven to broil and line a half sheet pan with aluminum foil. Place an oven-safe wire rack in the sheet pan, then place the wings on the wire rack.

- Pour the leftover sauce that's in the slow cooker into a medium sauce pan over medium-high heat. Whisk together the cornstarch and 2 tablespoons of water in a small bowl and stir in with the sauce. Simmer for 5 minutes stirring occasionally until the sauce thickens.

- Brush the wings with the sauce and place in the oven. Cook for 4-5 minutes until the sauce starts to bubble. Remove from the oven, flip the wings over, then brush with the sauce and place back in the oven for 4-5 minutes until the sauce is bubbly.

PIZZA DIP

SERVINGS: 20-24

This party food is a pizza lover's dream and goes perfectly with garlic bread or chips.

INGREDIENTS

- 16oz cream cheese
- 4 cups mozzarella cheese, shredded
- 1 cup Parmesan cheese, shredded
- 1/4 cup sour cream
- 14oz jar pizza sauce
- 1 bell pepper, diced
- 5oz bag mini pepperonis
- Fresh basil, chopped

DIRECTIONS

Add the cream cheese, mozzarella cheese, Parmesan cheese, sour cream, pizza sauce, bell pepper, and pepperonis to the slow cooker. Cook on low for 3 hours or high for 1-1/2 hours, stirring occasionally. Garnish with basil and serve with garlic bread or tortilla chips.

TACO SOUP

SERVINGS: 6-8

This hearty and filling party favorite will have people fighting for the last spoonful.
A ton of flavors that marry perfectly together.

INGREDIENTS

- 2lbs ground beef, browned and drained
- 1 medium onion, diced
- 1 red bell pepper, diced
- 1 jalapeño pepper, diced (seeded for less heat)
- 3 garlic cloves, minced
- 14.5oz can diced tomatoes
- 14.5oz can whole kernel corn, drained
- 14.5oz can kidney beans, drained
- 1 package taco seasoning
- 1 teaspoon chili powder
- 1/2 teaspoon paprika
- 1 teaspoon salt
- 1/2 teaspoon black pepper
- 3 cups beef stock
- Fresh cilantro, chopped
- Sharp cheddar cheese, shredded
- Sour cream

DIRECTIONS

Add the ground beef, onion, bell pepper, jalapeño pepper, garlic, tomatoes, corn, kidney beans, taco seasoning, chili powder, paprika, salt, black pepper, and beef stock to the slow cooker. Cook on low for 6 hours or on high for 4 hours. Top with cilantro, cheese, and sour cream. Serve with tortilla chips.

CHICKEN MARSALA

SERVINGS: 4

A classic Italian-American dish that envelopes tender chicken and mushrooms with a rich marsala wine sauce.

INGREDIENTS

- 4 boneless, skinless chicken breasts
- Salt
- Black pepper
- Olive oil
- 1 small onion, diced
- 1 cup mushrooms, sliced
- 1-1/2 teaspoons fresh thyme, chopped
- 4 garlic cloves, minced
- 1 cup marsala wine
- 1 cup chicken stock
- 1/4 cup corn starch
- 1/4 cup heavy cream
- Fresh parsley, roughly chopped

DIRECTIONS

- Season the chicken breasts with salt and pepper. Add 2 tablespoons of olive oil to a pan or skillet over medium heat. Once the oil is hot, cook the chicken 2-3 minutes each side until slightly browned. Remove the chicken and place in a greased bowl of a slow cooker.

- Add 1 more tablespoon of olive oil to the pan, then add the onions, mushrooms, thyme, 1 teaspoon salt, and 1 teaspoon black pepper and cook until tender, about 5 minutes. Add in the garlic and cook for 1 minute. Stir in the marsala wine, scraping the browned bits at the bottom of the pan. Stir in the chicken stock and remove the pan from the heat. Pour the mixture over top of the chicken and place the lid on the slow cooker.

- Cook on low for 4-5 hours or high for 2-3 hours.

- Turn the slow cooker to high. In a small bowl, whisk together the corn starch and 1/2 cup water and add to the slow cooker. Add in the heavy cream. Cook for 20-30 minutes until the sauce thickens. Serve hot garnished with parsley.

SLOW COOKED BBQ RIBS

SERVINGS: 2-3

These ribs are slow cooked until they're fall-off-the-bone tender.
These succulent, delicious ribs require just a few ingredients and even fewer steps.

INGREDIENTS

- 1/2 cup brown sugar
- 1 tablespoon fresh rosemary, chopped
- 2 teaspoons paprika
- 2 teaspoons garlic powder
- 1/4 teaspoon cumin
- 1/4 teaspoon red pepper flakes
- Salt & black pepper to taste
- 3lbs baby back pork ribs
- 2 cups BBQ sauce

DIRECTIONS

- In a small bowl, mix together the brown sugar, rosemary, paprika, garlic powder, cumin, red pepper flakes, and salt and black pepper. Spread the rub all over the ribs.

- Add the ribs to the slow cooker topped with the BBQ sauce and cook on low for 8 hours or high for 4 hours. When done, spoon the BBQ sauce over the ribs.

BREAD MACHINE

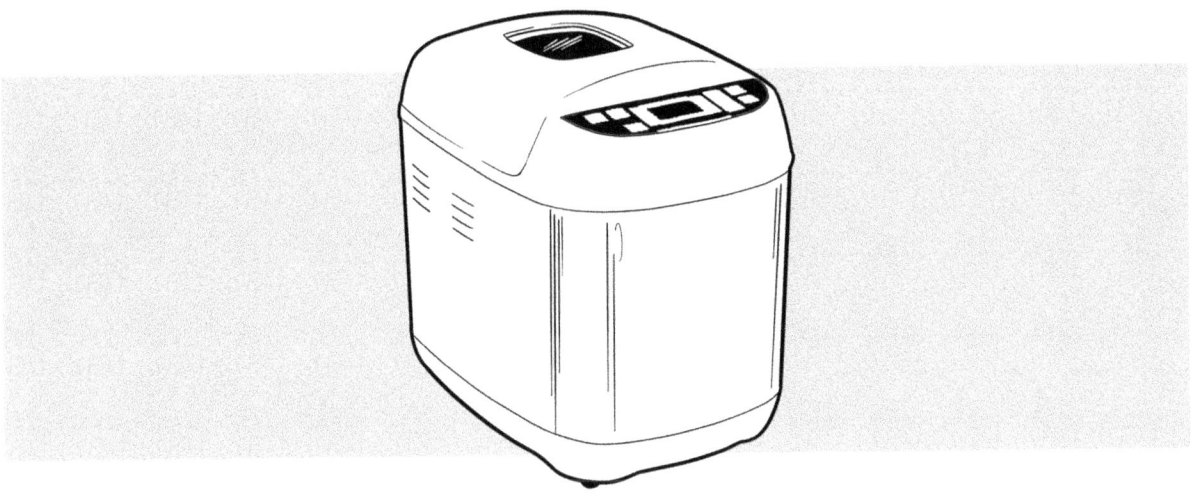

People have been making bread for thousands of years. Nothing can compare to a homemade kneaded-by-hand loaf of bread, but who has that kind of time nowadays? A bread machine makes that process so much easier.

Several years ago, my parents got me a bread machine for Christmas. I didn't know much about making bread from scratch, so it got pushed to the back of my cabinet and was rarely used. Later, I decided to put it to use and start experimenting with making bread from scratch. What a difference a fresh loaf of bread makes! I now make a loaf of bread at least once a week.

Making bread from scratch sounds difficult and time-consuming, but with a bread machine the process couldn't be easier. For most loaves, you literally throw the ingredients in the machine, press start, and walk away. The machine even does the proving and baking for you. A bread machine allows even the most novice of bakers to create amazing homemade bread.

A bread machine can do more than knead and bake a loaf of bread. Most have several different functions and cycles that can make all kinds of doughs, rolls, buns, even cakes and jams.

Many recipes start and end in the bread machine, always giving you the same square loaf shape. A lot of times, I like to make the dough in the machine, then shape and score the bread into more "homemade" looking loaves and bake them in the oven. You'll be amazed at how easy it is to make homemade bread with the help of a bread machine. The bread machine is perfect for kneading the dough, especially for people who have physical issues like arthritis where kneading bread by hand would be almost impossible.

I've included the weight of the ingredients because it's very important to measure out the ingredients when making bread to get a consistent loaf every time.

WHITE BREAD

MAKES: 1.5lb Loaf

TOOLS OF THE TRADE

Digital Scale: Easily and accurately measure the exact weight of ingredients.

Homemade bread that is so easy to make with the help of a bread machine!
This soft and delicious loaf can go with literally any meal. So much better than store-bought bread!

INGREDIENTS

- 2-1/4 teaspoons (7 grams) rapid-rise yeast
- 3 cups (408 grams) bread flour
- 2 tablespoons (25 grams) sugar
- 1-1/2 teaspoons (9 grams) salt
- 3 tablespoons (60 grams) unsalted butter (room temperature)
- 1 cup (240 grams) warm water (110 degrees)

DIRECTIONS

- Add the ingredients in order as listed to the bread machine. Set the cycle to basic/white bread for 1.5lb loaf and press start.

- When the bread is done, remove the bowl from the machine and let sit for 5 minutes. Turn the loaf out onto a wire rack to cool.

100% WHOLE WHEAT BREAD

MAKES: 1.5lb Loaf

This hearty and delectable bread is easy to make with a bread machine.
A healthier alternative to white bread.

INGREDIENTS

- 1-1/4 teaspoons (4 grams) rapid-rise yeast
- 3 cups (390 grams) whole wheat flour
- 1-1/2 teaspoons (9 grams) salt
- 1/4 cup (85 grams) honey
- 3 tablespoons (60 grams) unsalted butter (room temperature)
- 1 egg (50 grams), room temperature
- 1-1/4 cups (59 grams) lukewarm water (80-90 degrees)

DIRECTIONS

- Add the ingredients in order as listed to the bread machine. Set the cycle to whole wheat for 1.5lb loaf and press start.

- When the bread is done, remove the bowl from the machine and let sit for 5 minutes. Turn the loaf out onto a wire rack to cool.

BLUEBERRY BREAD

MAKES: 1.5lb Loaf

A super-moist bread that's loaded with fresh blueberries for that perfectly sweet loaf.

INGREDIENTS

- 2 teaspoons (6 grams) rapid-rise yeast
- 3 cups (408 grams) bread flour
- 1 teaspoon (6 grams) salt
- 1/2 cup (100 grams) light brown sugar
- 1 egg (50 grams), room temperature
- 1/2 cup (110 grams) unsalted butter (room temperature)
- 1 teaspoon (4 grams) vanilla extract

- Zest of 1 lemon
- 3/4 cup (168 grams) warm whole milk (70-80 degrees)
- 1 cup (148 grams) fresh blueberries

Glaze:
- 1 cup confectioners' sugar
- 2 tablespoons whole milk
- 1/4 teaspoon vanilla extract

DIRECTIONS

- Add the yeast, flour, salt, brown sugar, egg, butter, vanilla extract, lemon zest, and milk to the bowl of the bread machine and set the cycle to basic/white bread for 1.5lb loaf and press start. When the "Add In" signal sounds, add in the blueberries. When the cycle is done, remove the bread and let cool to room temperature.

- For the glaze, whisk together the confectioners' sugar, milk, and vanilla extract until smooth. Pour the glaze over the warm bread.

MAPLE OATMEAL BREAD

MAKES: 1.5lb Loaf

This golden loaf has just the right amount of sweetness from the maple syrup.
Great to serve for breakfast or a sweet snack.

INGREDIENTS

- 2-1/4 teaspoons (7 grams) rapid-rise yeast
- 3 cups (408 grams) bread flour
- 2 tablespoons (25 grams) sugar
- 1-1/2 teaspoons (9 grams) salt
- 1-1/2 teaspoons (4 grams) ground cinnamon
- 1/2 cup (39 grams) oats, plus more for topping
- 2 eggs (100 grams), room temperature
- 1/2 cup (110 grams) pure maple syrup
- 1/2 cup (110 grams) unsalted butter, melted
- 1 cup (225 grams) buttermilk

DIRECTIONS

- Add all the ingredients in order as listed to the bread machine. Set to the sweet cycle at 1.5lb loaf and press start. After the kneading cycle is done, sprinkle the top of the dough with oats.

- When the bread is done, remove the loaf from the pan and place on a wire rack to cool completely.

PUMPKIN BREAD

MAKES: 1.5lb Loaf

This fall favorite bread is packed with cinnamon and spice.
The perfect complement to a hot cup of coffee on a crisp autumn day.

INGREDIENTS

- 1/2 cup (110 grams) unsalted butter, melted
- 1 cup (225 grams) pumpkin puree
- 2 eggs (100 grams), room temperature
- 2 teaspoons (9 grams) vanilla extract
- 1 cup (213 grams) brown sugar
- 2 cups (120 grams) all-purpose flour
- 1 teaspoon (4 grams) baking powder
- 1 teaspoon (4 grams) baking soda
- 1 teaspoon (6 grams) salt
- 1 teaspoon (3 grams) ground cinnamon
- 1/2 teaspoon (3 grams) nutmeg
- 1/4 teaspoon (0.5 grams) all spice
- 1/4 teaspoon (1 gram) ground ginger

DIRECTIONS

Add all the ingredients in order as listed to the pan of the bread machine. Set to the sweet cycle for 1.5lb loaf and press start. When the bread is done, remove the loaf from the pan and place on a wire rack to cool completely.

JALAPEÑO CHEDDAR BREAD

MAKES: 1.5lb Loaf

This deliciously savory bread has the perfect blend of flavor with the spicy jalapeños and the sharp cheddar cheese.

INGREDIENTS

- 2-1/4 teaspoons (7 grams) rapid-rise yeast
- 3 cups (408 grams) bread flour
- 1 tablespoon (12.5 grams) sugar
- 1-1/2 teaspoons (9 grams) salt
- 3 tablespoons (60 grams) unsalted butter (room temperature)
- 1 cup (225 grams) buttermilk
- 1 cup (120 grams) cheddar cheese, shredded
- 1/4 cup jalapeño peppers, seeded and diced

DIRECTIONS

- Add the yest, flour, sugar, salt, butter, and buttermilk to the bread machine and set the cycle to basic/white for 1.5lb loaf and press start. When the "Add-In" signal sounds, add the cheese and jalapeño peppers.

- When the bread is done, remove the bowl from the machine and let sit for 5 minutes. Turn the loaf out onto a wire rack to cool.

GARLIC & HERB KNOTS

MAKES: 12 Knots

Amazingly soft bread knots packed with garlic and herb flavor.
All it needs is a good slather of marinara sauce and you'll be in carb heaven!

INGREDIENTS

- 2-1/4 teaspoons (7 grams) rapid-rise yeast
- 3 cups (408 grams) bread flour
- 1 teaspoon (5 grams) sugar
- 1-1/2 teaspoons (9 grams) salt
- 6 tablespoons (85 grams) unsalted butter (room temperature)
- 1 cup water (240 grams), room temperature
- 1/3 cup (57 grams) Parmesan cheese, grated
- 1 tablespoon (3 grams) fresh thyme, chopped
- 1 tablespoon (2 grams) fresh rosemary, chopped
- 1 tablespoon (1 gram) fresh basil, chopped
- 2 garlic cloves, minced

Topping:

- 4 tablespoons unsalted butter
- 1 teaspoon fresh thyme, chopped
- 1 teaspoon fresh basil, chopped
- 2 garlic cloves, minced
- Grated Parmesan cheese

DIRECTIONS

- Add all the ingredients for the dough to the bowl of the bread machine as listed and select the dough cycle.

- When the cycle is done, transfer the dough to a flat surface and divide the dough into 12 equal pieces. Roll each piece into a rope about 10 inches long, then loosely tie into a knot. Place the knots onto a baking sheet lined with parchment paper then cover and let the dough rest for 30 minutes.

- Preheat the oven to 375 degrees.

- For the topping, melt the butter in a small saucepan, then stir in the thyme, basil, and garlic. Brush each knot with the butter mixture. Bake in the oven for 15-20 minutes until the knots are lightly browned. Remove from the oven and immediately brush with reserved melted butter and top with Parmesan cheese.

GLAZED DONUTS

TOOLS OF THE TRADE

MAKES: 9-11 Donuts & Donut Holes

Multiple Mixing Bowls:
One can never have enough of
these multi-functional bowls.

*The ultimate dessert! These perfectly light and fluffy
donuts slathered in a sweet sticky glaze is the
very definition of heaven. Bet you can't eat just one!*

INGREDIENTS

- 2-1/4 teaspoons (7 grams) rapid-rise yeast
- 3 cups (384 grams) all-purpose flour
- 1/2 cup (100 grams) sugar
- 1/4 teaspoon (2 grams) salt
- 1 egg (50 grams), room temperature
- 1 egg yolk (18 grams), room temperature
- 1-1/2 teaspoons (2 grams) vanilla extract

- 1/4 cup (57 grams) unsalted butter, melted
- 3/4 cup (184 grams) warm whole milk (100 degrees)
- 48oz vegetable oil

Glaze:
- 2 cups confectioners' sugar, sifted
- 1 teaspoon vanilla extract
- 1/4 cup whole milk

DIRECTIONS

- Add the yeast, flour, sugar, salt, eggs, vanilla extract, butter, and warmed milk to the bowl of the bread machine and set to the dough cycle, then press start.

- Once the cycle is done, punch down the dough, then transfer to a lightly floured surface. Using a rolling pin lightly dusted with flour, roll the dough to 1/2-inch thickness. Cut the donuts out with a biscuit cutter, then cut out the center of each donut with a smaller cutter. Place the donuts and donut holes on a sheet pan lined with parchment paper, then cover and let rise for 40 minutes.

- Add the vegetable oil to a large pot over medium-high heat. When the oil reaches 350 degrees with a candy thermometer, fry the donuts and donut holes in batches until golden brown, about 1-2 minute on each side. Cool on a sheet pan lined with a cooling rack.

- For the glaze, whisk together the confectioners' sugar, vanilla extract, and milk in a small pot until combined. Place the pot over low heat and stir occasionally until the glaze is heated through. Remove from the heat and then dip each donut and donut hole in the glaze and set back on the cooling rack.

BUTTERMILK WHOLE WHEAT DINNER ROLLS

MAKES: 12 Rolls

These soft, rustic dinner rolls topped with melted butter, are the perfect starter to any dinner.

INGREDIENTS

- 2-1/4 teaspoons (7 grams) rapid rise yeast
- 1-1/2 cups (195 grams) whole wheat flour
- 1-1/2 cups (194 grams) bread flour
- 1/4 cup (50 grams) brown sugar
- 1-1/2 teaspoons (9 grams) salt
- 1 egg (50 grams), room temperature
- 2 tablespoons (28 grams) sour cream
- 1 cup (225 grams) buttermilk

DIRECTIONS

- Add the ingredients in order as listed to the machine. Set to the dough cycle and press start.

- Line a half-sheet pan with parchment paper.

- When the cycle is done, dump the dough out onto a floured surface, divide the dough into 12 equal pieces, and place on the sheet pan. Cover the pan with a towel or loose plastic wrap and let rise in a warm place for 45 minutes.

- Preheat the oven to 375 degrees. Bake the rolls for 18-20 minutes until golden brown.

DINNER ROLLS

MAKES: 18-20 Rolls

Let's face it, everyone's favorite part of a meal is the bread. These heavenly, soft, buttery rolls are a must with any dinner.

INGREDIENTS

- 2-1/4 teaspoons (7grams) rapid-rise yeast
- 3-1/2 cups (476 grams) bread flour
- 3 tablespoons (42 grams) sugar
- 1 teaspoon (6 grams) salt
- 1/2 cup (110 grams) unsalted butter (room temp)
- 2 eggs (100 grams), room temperature
- 1 cup (240 grams) warm whole milk (80-90 degrees)

DIRECTIONS

- Add the ingredients in order as listed to the machine. Set to the dough cycle and press start.

- Preheat the oven to 350 degrees and line a sheet pan with parchment paper.

- When the cycle is done, dump the dough onto a cutting board. Cut the dough into 2-inch pieces and place on the sheet pan. Bake for 15-20 minutes until rolls are lightly browned. Top with butter and/or honey.

MILK & HONEY BREAD

MAKES: 1.5lb Loaf

This deliciously light, sweet bread is perfect for any sandwich.

INGREDIENTS

- 2-1/4 teaspoons (7 grams) rapid-rise yeast
- 3 cups (408 grams) bread flour
- 1 teaspoon (6 grams) salt
- 2 eggs (100 grams) divided, room temperature
- 2 tablespoons (28 grams) unsalted butter (room temperature)
- 3 tablespoons (60 grams) honey
- 1 cup (225 grams) buttermilk
- Sesame seeds

DIRECTIONS

- Add the yeast, flour, salt, 1 egg, butter, honey, and buttermilk to the bread machine. Set to the dough cycle and press start.

- Preheat the oven to 375 degrees.

- When the cycle is done, place the dough into a greased loaf pan or form into the shape of a loaf and place on a sheet pan lined with parchment paper. Whisk together 1 egg and 1 tablespoons of water in a small bowl. Brush the top of the dough with the egg wash, then sprinkle on sesame seeds. Bake for 25-30 minutes until golden brown.

PEANUT BUTTER BREAD

MAKES: 1.5lb Loaf

The perfect grab-and-go breakfast bread.

INGREDIENTS

- 2-1/4 teaspoon (7 grams) rapid-rise yeast
- 3 cups (408 grams) bread flour
- 1/2 teaspoon (3 grams) salt
- 1/4 cup (50 grams) brown sugar
- 1 cup (250 grams) peanut butter
- 1 egg (50 grams), room temperature
- 4 tablespoons (57 grams) unsalted butter (room temperature)
- 1 teaspoon (4 grams) vanilla extract
- 1-1/4 cup (59 grams) warm water (110 degrees)

DIRECTIONS

Add the ingredients in order as listed to the bread machine. Set the cycle to basic/white bread for 1.5lb loaf and press start. When the bread is done, remove the bowl from the machine and let sit for 5 minutes. Turn the loaf out onto a wire rack to cool.

SOURDOUGH BREAD

MAKES: 1 Loaf

Rustic, crusty sourdough bread that's simple and easy to make.

INGREDIENTS

- 3/4 cup sourdough starter (pg 196)
- 3 cups (408 grams) bread flour
- 1-1/2 teaspoons (9 grams) salt
- 1/2 teaspoon (2 grams) sugar
- 1 cup (240 grams) lukewarm water
- Cornmeal

DIRECTIONS

- Place all the ingredients in the bread machine in order as listed and set to the dough cycle. Once the cycle is complete, let the dough rest in the bread machine or at room temperature for 3 hours.

- Gently knead the dough into an oval loaf and place on parchment paper sprinkled with cornmeal. Wrap the top of the dough with plastic wrap that has been lightly greased with cooking spray. Place in the refrigerator for 8-16 hours.

- Place a sheet pan in the oven, then preheat to 450 degrees.

- Remove the plastic wrap from the dough, then lightly dust the top of the dough with flour. Score the top of the dough with a sharp paring knife.

- Place the dough on the parchment paper on the hot sheet pan from the oven. Bake for 45 minutes until golden brown, then remove from the oven and let cool completely before slicing.

SOURDOUGH STARTER

Easy sourdough starter made right at home.

You can't make sourdough bread without sourdough starter. Basically, sourdough starter is a live fermented culture of flour and water that makes the bread rise.

Creating a starter is not only an art, but also a science. An entire book can be dedicated to sourdough starters. When learning how to make a starter, I quickly became overwhelmed at the process. Making a sourdough starter is actually very easy, but it does require time and patience.

The following recipe is an easy beginner sourdough starter that requires a small amount of time and effort. A digital scale is very important for this to ensure consistency.

INGREDIENTS

- 20g rye flour
- 30g unbleached all-purpose flour
- 50g lukewarm water

TOOLS

- Digital scale
- Glass jar with loose-fitting lid

FEEDING ROUTINE

- **Day 1:** Add 20g rye flour, 30g all-purpose flour, and 50g lukewarm water to a jar with a loose lid and stir with a fork until well incorporated. Place at room temperature.

- **Day 2:** Do nothing. You may see small bubbles appear on the surface. Rest the starter for another 24 hours.

- **Day 3:** Discard half of the starter then weigh in 20g rye flour, 30g all-purpose flour, and 50g lukewarm water to the remaining starter in the jar and stir with a fork until well incorporated. Loosely place the lid on and set at room temperature.

- **Day 4-7:** Repeat the steps from day 3. As you feed the starter each day, you will begin to see large bubbles appear and the starter rising and falling. By the seventh day the starter should look spongey, have doubled in size, and have a sour smell.

- **Note:** The starter isn't always ready on the seventh day. Due to factors such as temperature and timing, it could take up to two weeks before the starter is ready. If your starter is not ready by the seventh day, continue the daily feeding process until the floating test works.

FLOATING TEST

To check to see if the starter is ready to bake with, place about 1 tablespoon of the starter in a glass of water. If the starter floats, the starter is ready. If the starter sinks, the starter is not ready. If the starter is not ready, continue to feed until the it floats.

STORING & MAINTAINING STARTER

Once you have created your starter, you can either store it at room temperature or in the refrigerator.

- **If storing at room temperature:** discard half of the starter and feed with 20g rye flour, 30g all-purpose flour, and 50g lukewarm water daily.

- **If storing in the refrigerator:** discard half of the starter and feed with 20g rye flour, 30g all-purpose flour, and 50g lukewarm water weekly.

- **Note:** When preparing to bake with starter from the refrigerator, feed the starter and set at room temperature for 4-8 hours until bubbly.

Italian
Seasoning

Brown Sugar

White Rice

Tone's

black
Pepper
restaurant

PIMIENTA NEGRA
TIPO RESTAURANTE

Kosher
Salt

MORTON
IODIZED SALT

DELALLO
INSTANT
ESPRESSO

HERSHEY'S
COCOA
100% CACAO
NATURAL UNSWEETENED

ARGO
100% PURE
CORN STARCH

Fleischmann's
Bread Machine

MAGNUM

GROUND SAIGON
CINNAMON

Baker's

Graham Cracker Crumbs

Lake Gaston
Coffee

Cake Flour

Wegmans
100% Mediterranean Blend
OLIVE OIL
EXTRA VIRGIN

33.8 FL OZ (1 QT 1.8 FL OZ) 1 L

A well-stocked pantry is a must! If you have the basic pantry items on hand, you'll find it's easy to whip up recipes because you'll already have most of the ingredients ready to go. Listed are the pantry items I always have stocked because I use them most often and how long they will last.

SPICES — keeps for 6 months

- All Spice
- Basil
- Bay Leaves
- Black Pepper
- Black Peppercorns
- Cayenne Pepper
- Chili Powder
- Cinnamon
- Coriander, ground
- Cream of Tartar
- Cumin
- Garlic Powder
- Ginger
- Italian Seasoning
- Nutmeg
- Onion Powder
- Paprika
- Red Pepper Flakes
- Oregano
- Sage
- Salt (table and Kosher)

BAKING — keeps for...

Item	keeps for...
Baking Powder	6 months to a year
Baking Soda	8 months to a year
Brown Sugar	3 to 4 months
Cornstarch	Indefinitely
Cocoa Powder	1 to 2 years
Confectioners' Sugar	Indefinitely (sealed)
Flour (all-purpose, bread, cake)	1 year (sealed)
Sugar (granulated)	Indefinitely (sealed)
Vanilla Extract	1 to 2 years
Yeast (rapid rise)	1 to 2 years

MISCELLANEOUS — refer to package for expiration

- Bread Crumbs (plain, Italian, Panko)
- Dried Pasta
- Honey
- Molasses
- Oil (extra virgin and vegetable)
- Rice (white and brown)
- Store Bought Stock (chicken and beef)
- Vinegar (cider and balsamic)

KITCHEN CONVERSIONS

ORIGINAL	SUBSTITUTE
almond extract (1/2 tsp)	vanilla extract (3/4 tsp)
baking powder (1 tsp)	1/4 tsp baking soda + 1/2 tsp cwh milk for 1 cup
buttermilk (1 cup)	3 tbsp unsweet cocoa pwdr + 1-1/2 tbsp granulated sugar + 1-1/2 tsp butter oil
chocolate, semi-sweet (~1/3 cup)	1-1/4 cup granulated sugar, dissolve in 1/4 cup hot water
corn syrup (1 cup)	1 tsp dried oregano + 1/2 tsp dried basil + 1/2 tsp dried thyme
Italian seasoning (2 tsp)	1/2 tsp cinnamon + 1/4 tsp gnd nutmeg + 1/4 tsp gnd ginger + 1/2 tsp gnd cloves
pumpkin pie spice (1 tsp)	1 cup granulated sugar + 2 to 3 tbsp molasses
sugar, dark brown (1 cup)	1 cup granulated sugar + 1 to 2 tbsp molasses
sugar, light brown (1 cup)	1/2 cup + 1-1/2 tbsp granulated sugar + 3/4 tsp corn starch, finely ground in blender
sugar, powdered (~1 cup)	2 to 3 tbsp tomato purée or tomato sauce, boil to 1 tbsp
tomato paste (1 tbsp)	2 to 3 tsp vanilla extract
vanilla bean (8" pod)	

SPOONS & CUPS

TEASPOONS	TABLESPOONS	CUPS
3 tsp	1 tbsp	1/16 cup
6 tsp	2 tbsp	1/8 cup
12 tsp	4 tbsp	1/4 cup
18 tsp	6 tbsp	1/3 cup
24 tsp	8 tbsp	1/2 cup
36 tsp	12 tbsp	3/4 cup
48 tsp	16 tbsp	1 cup

LIQUID EQUIVALENTS

1 cup	8 ounces
1 pint	2 cups 16 ounces
1 quart	4 cups 32 ounces
1 gallon	4 quarts 128 ounces

TEMPERATURE

FAHRENHEIT	CELSIUS
250° F	121° C
300° F	149° C
325° F	163° C
350° F	177° C
375° F	190° C
400° F	204° C
425° F	218° C
450° F	232° C
475° F	246° C
500° F	260° C

My First Thanksgiving

Everyone wants to be happy. Happiness these days seems to be measured in money or success, but I think at the end of the day, it's the little things that make us truly happy. My ultimate happiness is sitting around my supper table with my loved ones.

While all of the cookware and equipment in this book are important for a great kitchen, I think the most important kitchen essential is the supper table.

A supper table is a place where family and friends get together to laugh, cry, and enjoy memorable meals. It doesn't have to be a big, expensive, grandiose thing, just a simple table to gather with the people who are most important to you. It is without a doubt the center of the household.

I'm fortunate enough to have inherited my grandparents' supper table. I have so many amazing memories at that table that I wouldn't trade anything for and I love making new ones.

Whether it's a big holiday meal with family and friends gathered around or if it's just Brad and I watching TV while eating greasy Chinese take-out, it's honestly my favorite place in my house and it's my ultimate kitchen essential.

My Grandparent's Kitchen Table...
Always Dressed To Impress

RECIPE
QUICK GUIDE

RECEIPE
QUICK GUIDE

EVERYDAY KITCHEN
ESSENTIALS

Author: Steven Baker
Cover Photography: Ashley Wall
Artwork: David Chiu
Edited by: James Kinard & Susan Rehm
Graphic Designer: Lisa Kludy

For more recipes, please visit:
www.stevendoesfood.com

Also by Steven Baker:
**Everyday
Southern Comforts**